Jesus
through the
Old Testament

Transform your Bible understanding

Graeme Goldsworthy

BRF
Ministries

These are a shadow of the things to come, but the substance belongs to Christ.

COLOSSIANS 2:17

The Old Testament can be confusing or problematic for many readers. But in this book, Graeme Goldsworthy helps the Christian reader join the dots, and so make sense of the Old Testament's big picture. He shows how understanding the Old Testament comes from seeing it as a witness to the person and work of Jesus Christ. Goldsworthy traces the developing idea of the kingdom of God through the Old Testament, neatly summarised by his maxim, 'God's people in God's place under God's rule'. Readers will appreciate his explanation of fulfilment and typology, supporting ideas, his explanation of example texts, and the sense of movement towards Jesus. Rather than focus on details that might overwhelm the beginner, Goldsworthy provides a basic roadmap for how the Old Testament's big ideas, from Genesis to Malachi, find their ultimate meaning in Jesus Christ.

**George Athas, Director of Postgraduate Studies,
Moore Theological College, Sydney**

No one has done more in the past 50 years to contribute to the recovery of Biblical Theology for the church than Graeme Goldsworthy. Now in this crystal-clear, deeply practical and enormously helpful book, Graeme has condensed years of reflection on and teaching of the Bible for the benefit of the church. I can think of no more helpful place to start for anyone who wants to find out how to read, understand and apply the message of the Bible. I pray that this book gets the attention and widespread use that it deserves for the sake of Christ and his kingdom.

Gary Millar, Principal, Queensland Theological College

BRF Ministries

15 The Chambers, Vineyard
Abingdon OX14 3FE
brf.org.uk

Bible Reading Fellowship is a charity (233280)
and company limited by guarantee (301324),
registered in England and Wales

ISBN 978 0 85746 567 2
First published 2017
All rights reserved

Acknowledgements
Unless otherwise stated, scripture quotations taken from the Holy Bible, English
Standard Version, published by HarperCollins Publishers, © 2001 Crossway Bibles,
a division of Good News Publishers. Used by permission. All rights reserved.

Scripture quotations taken from The Holy Bible, New International Version
(Anglicised edition) copyright © 1979, 1984, 2011 by Biblica. Used by permission
of Hodder & Stoughton Publishers, a Hachette UK company. All rights reserved.
'NIV' is a registered trademark of Biblica. UK trademark number 1448790.

Extracts from the Authorised Version of the Bible (The King James Bible), the rights
in which are vested in the Crown, are reproduced by permission of the Crown's
Patentee, Cambridge University Press.

Scripture quotations from The Revised Standard Version of the Bible, copyright
© 1946, 1952, 1971 by the Division of Christian Education of the National Council
of the Churches of Christ in the United States of America. Used by per-mission.
All rights reserved.

Every effort has been made to trace and contact copyright owners for material
used in this resource. We apologise for any inadvertent omissions or errors, and
would ask those concerned to contact us so that full acknowledgement can be
made in the future.

A catalogue record for this book is available from the British Library

Contents

Foreword

I am so deeply grateful that I grew up going to Sunday school where I learned the stories of the Old Testament. I'm grateful that I was in Vacation Bible School every summer where we did things like make salt maps of the promised land and built the walls of Jericho out of Popsicle sticks. I am grateful for all of the history and doctrine I learned in my college Bible classes, for the personal challenges I got from reading Christian books over the years and for the expectation that God would speak to me and change me through his word that developed in the years I spent in an intensive weekly Bible study as an adult.

But as grateful as I am for all of those things, I realise that all of this immersion in the Bible left me with little to no understanding of how the Bible fits together as one story of God's outworking of his plan to redeem all things through Christ. I didn't know how to relate the curse and the promise given in Genesis 3 with everything that followed it. I couldn't have traced the story of Israel's exodus, entering the land, taking possession of the land, being exiled from the land and returning to the land. I couldn't have explained how the kingdom of Israel in the Old Testament relates to the kingdom Jesus announced at his coming. I looked at Old Testament characters as examples to follow or eschew and never imagined that Christ was prefigured in some of them. I simply avoided the Old Testament prophets because they were unintelligible and, in my mind, not anything I could apply to my real life in the here and now.

Fortunately, the day came when I began to be introduced to the way of grasping the larger story and the themes of the Bible as is introduced and explained in this book. When I discovered the teaching of Graeme Goldsworthy, the puzzle pieces began to fall into place. The Bible began to make sense to me in a new and profound way. More than that, Christ became more precious to me. Seeing who he is, and what he accomplished in his first coming, through the various angles of the Old Testament, added texture and colour.

How I wish I'd had a book like *Jesus through the Old Testament* long ago. I envy all who will become more thoroughly grounded in the contents, structure and meaning of the Bible much earlier than I was, through the pages of this book. As you work your way through it, you will be equipped to recognise important themes that run from beginning to end in the Bible. You'll see how the Old Testament points to a righteous life and the need for someone to provide it for us. Rather than approaching the Bible as a handbook for life, or as merely a source of inspiration, you'll become oriented to look for the progression of the kingdom of God as well as grasp the implications for living now as a glad subject of King Jesus.

If you have spent a lifetime in the Bible, but recognise there are still gaps in your understanding, this book will help to close some of those gaps. And if you are new to the Bible, this book will ground you in the basics so that your foundations will be firm and strong in the truth of God's revelation of himself and his plans and purposes in this world.

There could be no better guide than Graeme Goldsworthy for the pathway toward a firmer grasp on God's word. My prayer for you as you begin this book is that you will grow to love Christ more as you see him through all of the scriptures as a result of your study through this book.

Nancy Guthrie

Part 1

Where's Jesus?

1

Is the Old Testament a Christian book?

Where's Wally? is the first of a series of books by Martin Handford that most people will be familiar with.[1] In looking at a series of pictures, the trick is to spot the man in the red and white striped shirt and beanie amidst the most complicated and detailed mass of very small figures drawn with great care and precision. Looking for Jesus in the Old Testament is something like looking for Wally, only more complex. Wally can be found; he *is* there. But in the Old Testament, Jesus is not actually there in person as the Jesus we meet in the four Gospels.

Jesus of Nazareth comes along only after the Old Testament age finishes. So, if Jesus is there we need to understand *how* he is there. Before we even begin the search, there are many who would pose the question: 'Is the Old Testament really a Christian book?' You might be tempted to answer with a firm 'No' on the grounds that Jesus of Nazareth is nowhere mentioned by name in it. Others might reject it because it seems to focus on a very different religion from the Christianity we know. You may even regard Israel's religion as directly opposing the faith of the New Testament. One could easily feel that reading the Old Testament is rather like hitting your head against a brick wall; it feels good only when you stop. Bearing in mind that the Old Testament takes up about the first three-quarters of our Bible, dismissing it as irrelevant would save us a lot of time and effort.

What does the New Testament say about the matter?

But, of course, there is no way we can simply ignore the Old Testament; not when we start to read the New Testament and discover that the Old Testament, usually referred to as 'the scriptures', was the only Bible possessed and regularly used by Jesus and his apostles. Not only that, but they were consistent in the way they kept referring to the Old Testament as a book about Jesus. Consider, for example, the

> The Old Testament, usually referred to in the New Testament as 'the scriptures', was the only Bible used by Jesus and the first Christians.

different ways the four Gospels begin their Jesus-narratives by referring to some link with significant people or events in the Old Testament:

The book of the genealogy of Jesus Christ, the son of David, the son of Abraham.

MATTHEW 1:1

The beginning of the gospel of Jesus Christ, the Son of God. As it is written in Isaiah the prophet…

MARK 1:1–2

And the Lord God will give to him [Jesus] the throne of his father David, and he will reign over the house of Jacob for ever.

LUKE 1:32–33

In the beginning was the Word, and the Word was with God, and the Word was God. He was in the beginning with God. All things were made through him, and without him was not any thing made that was made. And the Word became flesh and dwelt among us.

> The four Gospels all begin by linking Jesus with the Old Testament.

JOHN 1:1–3, 14

The significance of these passages lies in the assumption that we need to understand the link with the Old Testament in order to understand Jesus:

- Matthew introduces Jesus as descended from David and Abraham, two of the most important characters in the Old Testament narrative.
- Mark says the gospel of Jesus Christ begins with the Old Testament prophets.
- Luke links Jesus with a key aspect of the history of Israel: the throne of David.
- John recalls the Genesis account of creation but asserts that Jesus, the Word, was the creator of all things.

Now see how Jesus himself spoke of his connection to the Old Testament ('the scriptures'):

> Then he said to them, 'These are my words that I spoke to you while I was still with you, that *everything written about me* in the Law of Moses and the Prophets and the Psalms must be fulfilled.' Then he opened their minds to understand the scriptures.
> LUKE 24:44–45[2]

> You search the scriptures because you think that in them you have eternal life; and it is *they that bear witness about me*, yet you refuse to come to me that you may have life.
> JOHN 5:39–40

> There is one who accuses you: Moses, on whom you have set your hope. For if you believed Moses, you would believe me; *for he wrote of me*.
> JOHN 5:45–46

Consider also what Paul says:

And we bring you the good news that what God promised to the fathers, this he has fulfilled to us their children by raising Jesus...
ACTS 13:32–33

Paul... [who has been] set apart for the gospel of God, which he promised beforehand through his prophets in the holy scriptures, concerning his Son, who was descended from David according to the flesh.
ROMANS 1:1–3

But now the righteousness of God has been manifested apart from the law, although the Law and the Prophets bear witness to it – the righteousness of God through faith in Jesus Christ for all who believe.
ROMANS 3:21–22

That will do for the moment: we could go on with many more New Testament passages, but the point is that the New Testament bears witness to the fact that the Old Testament is about Jesus. *How* it is about him is the question to which I will try to give some answers in this book. Everywhere we look in the New

> The whole of the New Testament bears witness to the fact that the Old Testament is about Jesus.

Testament we find quotes from the Old Testament or allusions to it. One estimate is that there are some 1,600 such places in the New Testament where the Old Testament is recalled, either directly by quotes or indirectly by references to its teachings and ideas.

These considerations alone are enough to explain why it is that the Christian church, from the very beginning of its history, has taken the Old Testament as its own scriptures. The Old Testament was the only Bible the first Christians

> If Jesus is the fulfiller then there is a real sense in which he is present in all the promises and expectations of the Old Testament.

had until the New Testament was written and accepted. The process of acceptance began with the apostles, but general acceptance of all 27 books of the New Testament may have been as late as the fifth century. However, the history of the church also shows us that a Christian interpretation of the Old Testament has always been, in various ways, a problem. So, from the beginning, Christians have struggled to make sense of the Old Testament. Nevertheless, it was never suggested by the church that we should abandon the Old Testament once the New Testament was received as scripture. The church has always acknowledged its sacred scriptures to consist of both Old and New Testaments.

Of course, it might be possible, without further reflection, to reduce the link between Jesus and the Old Testament simply to a historical one. It is claimed in the New Testament that Jesus is descended from the house of David of the Israelite tribe of Judah. However, that in itself does not establish any more of a relationship than one of lineage. There are millions of descendants from old Israel, but that does not make them the fulfillers of the Old Testament prophecies and promises. The significant point is that Jesus is proclaimed as the answer to all the expectations, prophetic predictions and divine promises of the Old Testament that are established by God himself. If this is the case, then there is a real sense in which Jesus is present in those promises and expectations. If Jesus is the fulfiller, it will help us greatly to understand exactly what it is that he fulfils.

I suggested at the outset that looking for Jesus in the Old Testament is more challenging than looking for Wally. I must now qualify that by saying that the greater difficulty exists for those who ignore the testimony of the New Testament. If we allow Jesus, the apostles and the other New Testament authors to guide us, we *will* find Jesus revealed in the Old Testament. It may not be in the way we expected, but he is there nevertheless.

Some false trails to avoid

There are some pitfalls to be avoided in our attempts to make use of the Old Testament in a consistently Christian way. And, as it is said, 'forewarned is forearmed'. Throughout the history of the Christian church, many unsatisfactory approaches have been tried and some of these are still around today. This is not the place to review the history of Old Testament interpretation, but we can avoid some of the less helpful approaches to the matter if we are aware of such pitfalls. Here are some possibilities to think about – but remember, the main purpose of this book is to propose some positive steps you can take towards a sound use of the Old Testament. The following approaches should be avoided:

1 The Old Testament is totally irrelevant to a Christian, so let's concentrate on the New Testament.

We can easily find ourselves taking this view by default. If we consider the Old Testament largely uninteresting, or difficult to understand, compared to the specifically Christian content of the New Testament, we could end up simply neglecting it. We may pay lip service to the idea that the whole Bible is God's word, but in reality we use only the New Testament. In practice, we will have jettisoned the Old Testament almost entirely.

2 The Old Testament is opposed to the New Testament because it deals with a failed programme of salvation through keeping the law.

This is a fatal misunderstanding. In the New Testament, there is a great deal about the good works we should do as believers. Most Christians recognise that such good works are the *fruit* of our free justification through faith, not the *cause* of it. There is a common misunderstanding of the Old Testament that the law of Moses is a programme of salvation by works of the law. We should be clear about the religion of the Old Testament: it *does not* set out a programme of salvation by works. It is not that God tried one way of salvation with Israel which failed, and so he had to devise another programme in the gospel. Both the New Testament

> The Old Testament is *not* a failed programme of salvation by works that God had to replace with the gospel.

and the Old Testament present a programme of salvation by grace through faith. The distinction is that, in the Old Testament, it is faith in the promises of God that are eventually fulfilled in Christ.

3 The Old Testament provides the examples of many godly people to imitate, and many evil people to avoid. Therefore, the moral example in the Old Testament is its only benefit.

There is no doubt that there are lots of godly and ungodly characters in the Old Testament. The problem is that using Old Testament characters only as examples often overlooks their behaviour in the wider context of what God is doing. *God is the principal character in the Old Testament*; our primary concern should be the acts of

> The main character in the Old Testament is God, not some human person or persons.

God, not the acts of human characters. None of the Old Testament characters are totally pure in what they do and say, neither are most totally evil. Thus, using these characters only as examples misses the bigger issue of their part in the progressive revelation of God's kingdom and of the way of salvation. If we focus exclusively on the human characters, we will overlook the fact that the main character in the narrative is not some Israelite hero (or anti-hero) but God himself.

To summarise:

- Some Christians see the Old Testament as plainly irrelevant.
- Some see the Old Testament as valuable for the moral examples, good or bad, of the characters in the narrative. That is, the Old Testament comes to be a book about ourselves.

- We have already seen that the New Testament understands the Old Testament as primarily a book about Christ. If we are to avoid the pitfalls, we need to develop a way of reading that reflects the New Testament's testimony to the Old Testament as a book about Christ.

In the next chapter, I will go on to consider what is involved in coming to a Christian mind on the Old Testament.

Key note

Jesus, the apostles, the New Testament writers and the early Christians all accepted the Old Testament as a book about Jesus Christ.

Take a moment to reflect…

- When you read the Old Testament, or hear it being read, do you ever ask yourself about how it points to Christ?
- When you read the New Testament, or hear it being read, do you ever reflect on the references to the Old Testament and why they are there?
- Have you ever wondered why our Bible includes the Old Testament?

Tip: Read Luke 24 and notice the links made between the resurrection of Jesus and the Old Testament.

2

Getting started:
looking at the big picture

We speak of the Bible as the word of God, and Jesus is also referred to as the Word of God who came in the flesh (John 1:1–3, 14). Doesn't that tell us something about the connection between Jesus and the whole Bible? In applying the title 'word' to both Jesus and the Bible, we are expressing the fact that the whole Bible is about Jesus.

Getting started with the Old Testament

So, let's be serious about the fact that we have a large book to deal with – in fact, a large collection of books. And we include all of them under the title of 'the word of God'. If Jesus is also the Word, our task is to understand the relationship between him and the Bible such that they both constitute the one word of God. Maybe you have never really handled the Old Testament before or, if you have, you may feel that you have not really understood what it is all about, or how it is relevant to your life. Where do we start? Well, one good way to become familiar with any book is first to look at the table of contents (if one is provided) and get a feeling for what it is all about. This table in your Bible will look something like the following. I have added comments in boxes in order to classify and describe the character of the 39 books that make up the Old Testament.

> If the Bible is the word of God and if Jesus is the Word of God, doesn't that suggest something about the connection between the two words?

The Old Testament

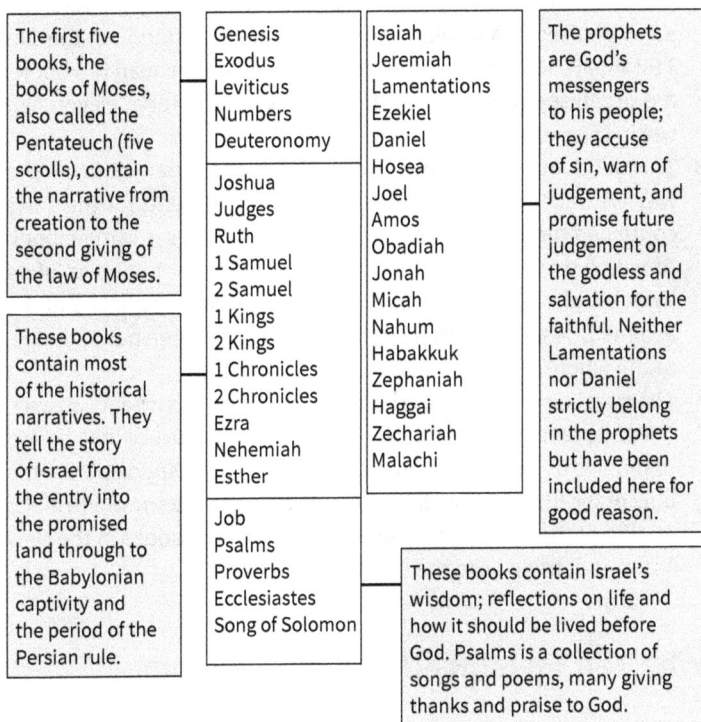

The first five books, the books of Moses, also called the Pentateuch (five scrolls), contain the narrative from creation to the second giving of the law of Moses.	Genesis Exodus Leviticus Numbers Deuteronomy	Isaiah Jeremiah Lamentations Ezekiel Daniel Hosea	The prophets are God's messengers to his people; they accuse of sin, warn of judgement, and promise future judgement on the godless and salvation for the faithful. Neither Lamentations nor Daniel strictly belong in the prophets but have been included here for good reason.
	Joshua Judges Ruth 1 Samuel 2 Samuel 1 Kings 2 Kings 1 Chronicles 2 Chronicles Ezra Nehemiah Esther	Joel Amos Obadiah Jonah Micah Nahum Habakkuk Zephaniah Haggai Zechariah Malachi	
These books contain most of the historical narratives. They tell the story of Israel from the entry into the promised land through to the Babylonian captivity and the period of the Persian rule.	Job Psalms Proverbs Ecclesiastes Song of Solomon	These books contain Israel's wisdom; reflections on life and how it should be lived before God. Psalms is a collection of songs and poems, many giving thanks and praise to God.	

Diagram 1: The books of the Old Testament

I am not going to include a table for the New Testament, as most people are more familiar with it. Its storyline is found in the four Gospels and the Acts of the Apostles. The remainder consists of letters written by apostles and others, most of them to various newly founded Christian churches.

Let me now summarise some basic facts about the Bible:

1   There are two main divisions called the Old Testament and the New Testament. We will come to the meaning of these names later.

2 In the Old Testament there are 39 books and in the New Testament there are 27, making 66 in all. Our English versions are organised in a similar way to the Greek translation of the Old Testament. It is not in chronological order, but instead the books are organised around their theme or type of writing, as you can see in Diagram 1 above.

3 The Jews organised their Hebrew Bible differently from the way we have it. The scriptures (the Old Testament) for the Jews contained three parts: Law, Prophets and Writings (the main book of which was Psalms).[3] So now you can see that in Luke 24:44 ('written about me in the Law of Moses and the Prophets and the Psalms'), Jesus is claiming to be related to all three parts, that is, to the whole of the Old Testament.

4 The question of when these books were written has no easy answer. The collection of 66 individual books was formed over a long period of time. If, as seems to be the case, Moses was responsible for the bulk of the first five books, we need to date them somewhere in the middle of the 15th century BC. The latest of the books in the New Testament bring us to the late first century AD.

Why 'Old Testament' and 'New Testament'?

'Testament' means the same as the biblical word 'covenant', both of which refer to a promise between God and humankind. Christians recognise that Jesus brings in a new covenant as the fulfilment of God's promises in the Old Testament. Thus, the Old Testament (Old Covenant) is essentially grounded on the promises of God and the New Testament (New Covenant) declares that these promises are fulfilled in Jesus Christ. Over the ages, Christians have used different ways of describing the relationship of the two Covenants, or Testaments.[4] The major contrast between the Testaments is that the Old Testament prepares for the coming of the Messiah (Saviour) and the New Testament proclaims the coming of Jesus as this expected Messiah, to live and die for his people.

The languages of the Bible

Three languages were used in the original biblical manuscripts.

- Hebrew is the language of most of the Old Testament books.
- Aramaic, a language closely related to Hebrew, is found in parts of Daniel and Ezra.
- Greek is the language of the New Testament.

The Israelites mostly spoke and wrote in an old Hebrew script similar to that used by the Canaanites. When the Jews (the southern kingdom of Judah) went into exile in Babylon between 597 and 586 BC, they learned to speak Aramaic, which was the language they encountered there. They also began to write their own language of Hebrew using the Aramaic alphabet.[5]

When we come to the time of Jesus, the Romans had replaced the Hellenistic Greek rulers of Judea, but common (or Koine) Greek was still the language used in that part of the Roman Empire. It is thought that Jesus probably spoke Aramaic, but the New Testament writers all used the more universal language of Greek.

The use of language

Every time you pick up a newspaper or your favourite magazine, you will easily recognise that there are many different ways we use language. You may never have consciously classified the different types of writing, but you will understand that we employ words in diverse ways to communicate. Not everything is a literal description of what has happened, or of what you expect to happen – that would be very boring. Reading the daily newspaper or a magazine requires us to adjust to many different kinds of writing. We usually do this without even thinking about it: we know that an editorial is not a news headline, nor is a comic strip or a classified advertisement.

It doesn't take long to realise that the Bible also contains a variety of literary types, and not all of these consist of literal description or narration. For example, although the Old Testament contains a single story of a people chosen by God to be his people, there is much more in the texts than story or historical narrative. We find:

- Laws and statutes
- Covenants
- Prophetic oracles
- Prayers
- Songs of praise, thanksgiving and lamentation
- Wisdom sayings
- Genealogies
- Parables and fables
- Poetic imagery: metaphor, simile and symbolism
- Apocalyptic visions and symbols

and much more.

In the same way that we adapt to different literary types in our daily reading (newspapers, books, magazines, blogs, tweets, etc.), so we should learn to adapt to the various kinds of biblical literature. Because the Bible is an ancient collection, it contains many genres or types of literature that we do not meet elsewhere in our daily lives. Many a curious doctrine has emerged from the readiness to read all biblical texts in the same way, often as completely literalistic narrative.

The unity of the Bible

This complexity might seem to make the business of reading the Bible very difficult and – let us be realistic about this – there are parts of the Bible which require some effort. Nevertheless, we

> We accept the unity of the Bible because Jesus and the apostles accepted the Old Testament as a book about Jesus Christ.

should not just say, 'It's all too hard!' and give up. I say this because there is a discernible structure to biblical revelation that all hangs on the storyline of God's redemptive history.

The unity of the Bible is something we believe because Jesus and his apostles clearly accepted that the Old Testament books, referred to as 'the scriptures', all come together in the person and work of Jesus himself. One difficulty for us is that this unity is not blindingly obvious when we read the Bible, partly because there is so much text to get our heads around. But we can be led by Jesus himself and his view of unity, which is that every part of the Old Testament points us to him; it is fulfilled in and by him. With this basic fact to guide us, it becomes much easier to begin to discern how all scripture is about Christ. Our sense of its unity will grow as we become more and more familiar with the Bible.

Conclusion

- The Old Testament is most definitely a Christian book. We are able to say this because Jesus, the apostles and other New Testament authors say it. The church has testified to this from the beginning.
- Christians are thus claiming that the Old Testament is, in itself, incomplete. Its true meaning is found only when it is linked to the New Testament.
- Since it is a Christian book testifying to Jesus, we as Christians should work hard to understand it as such.
- Some might argue that, since the Old Testament is fulfilled by the New Testament, we don't need to read it; we should read the New Testament because that is where the real substance is. However, this is short-sighted. If you don't know what the New Testament fulfils, you are less likely to understand it for what it is.

> The New Testament writers assume their readers have a knowledge of the Old Testament in what they say about Jesus as the fulfiller of it.

- Furthermore, the New Testament scriptures constantly refer to, quote, allude to and echo the Old Testament. They presuppose a knowledge of the Old Testament in its readers. There is so much in the New Testament that we simply cannot understand without knowing what is in the Old Testament. Whenever the New Testament refers to Jesus as 'the Christ',[6] it is pointing us to the Old Testament for an understanding of who and what the promised Christ (Messiah) is. Every time you refer to or use the title 'Christ' you are acknowledging the place of the Old Testament in our thinking.

We must now go on to consider how the Old Testament is constructed and in what way it testifies to Christ.

Key note
The overall 'big picture' implies a unity of the Old and New Testaments of the Bible, a unity that is endorsed by Jesus and the New Testament writers.

Take a moment to reflect…

- Read 2 Timothy 3:14–17. How does Paul describe the Old Testament and its role in Timothy's Christian life? What kind of unity in the Old Testament does he imply?
- A suggestion: take time to try to recall what you already know about the 'big picture' of the Bible.
- Spend a moment with the table of contents of the Old Testament and see if that helps you better appreciate the unity of the scriptures.

Tip: The big picture does not have to be full of detail; just get a sense of the Bible's main plot.

3

The storyline of the Bible

The Bible is built on a definite storyline. Like any good story it has a beginning, a middle and an end. The beginning is creation. The middle is the narrative of the history of Israel, leading to the central figure of Jesus of Nazareth. The end is the new creation and the kingdom of God. Other sections that aren't narrative are still related to the story of God's people because they were written by people who were part of that story and who reflect on the story.

Getting hold of the storyline

It is important that you first have some grasp of the big picture that is presented in the whole Bible, and avoid fragmentation that cuts off an event or a text from the wider context. The more you come to understand the big picture, the better you will be able to relate any part of it to the whole. I will say more about this when we come to look at specific parts of the Old Testament.

At this stage I want you to gain some confidence in knowing the broad sweep of the biblical narrative from creation to new creation. It is easy to become bogged down in some of the details, especially in the Old Testament. But if you concentrate on the main events, it is not so problematic. In the next chapter there is a condensed timeline which may be helpful to refer

> There is a coherent storyline in the Old Testament that runs from creation to the return of the Jews from the Babylonian exile.

back to in the future. Here is a suggested narrative outline of the key points in biblical revelation. The story goes something like this:

Outline of the Bible's story

God made everything including people, who disobeyed him and so came under the sentence of death. Things got very bad until God called Abraham and made some kind promises to him. But Abraham's descendants became slaves. God saved them and brought them, the nation of Israel, into the land originally promised to Abraham. God gave them a way to know him and be ruled by him. This involved the temple in Jerusalem and also the king. But things still were not good and Israel was finally thrown out of the land and into exile. Through his prophets, God told them why they were being judged. He also spoke words of comfort as he promised to save a faithful remnant of Israel and restore them as his people. But even the return from exile did not bring in the kingdom of God. After a long wait, Jesus came and declared that the kingdom 'is at hand'. He died for sinners and went to the Father. One day he will return to judge the living and the dead. The kingdom of God will then be universally seen in all its glory.

That's it in a nutshell, but I think we need a little more detail than that. So let's begin again and include a bit more of the story.

1 Beginnings: the creation narratives

- The Old Testament begins with two perspectives on creation (Genesis 1 and 2). Our first parents, Adam and Eve, are placed in the Garden of Eden with all that they need. They are, however, forbidden to eat from one certain, very special tree.

- The serpent emerges and tempts Eve to employ independence of thought; to think 'outside the square' of God's revelation. She involves Adam and they both fall for the temptation to be independent of God in assessing what truth is, and what is good and bad (Genesis 3). They are, in fact, taking it upon themselves to judge whether God can be trusted or not. They choose the negative.

- The threatened judgement of God falls and the couple are expelled from Eden; in an act of mercy, creation is made to fall with them so that the world is made fit for fallen people to live in. This might seem to be the end of the story, but God clearly has other ideas that cause him to pronounce a judgement on the serpent that includes the strong hint of a reversal of the fall (Genesis 3:15).

2 The progression of evil in the world

- The sons of Adam and Eve, Cain and Abel, are in dispute and, in anger, Cain kills his brother. From this point on there is the developing story of increasing evil in the world (Genesis 4—6). Finally, God declares that enough is enough, and determines to destroy humanity and the land-based animals in a great flood.

> It is important that you first grasp the big picture before trying to master the details.

- But God also has a purpose to save a few, and he chooses Noah and his family for salvation along with pairs of animals. In the ark, this one family floats to safety while all else is destroyed (Genesis 6—9).

- Two lines of people have emerged thus far: a godly line through Abel, Seth and Noah; and a godless line from Cain. Only Noah and his family survive the flood and events lead to a further similar distinction. Noah's three sons are now the forebears of three lines: a godless line through Ham; a godly line through Shem; and a 'piggy-back' line through Japheth that will somehow share Shem's blessings (Genesis 10—11).

3 The covenant of salvation

- Next, we are introduced to one of the most significant ideas and one of the most important figures in the biblical story: the covenant with Abraham

> The biblical story is about God himself; the Bible contains the acts of God.

(initially named Abram). As Noah had found grace (or favour) in the eyes of the Lord, so now Abram is chosen to receive a blessing of eternal significance (Genesis 11).

- God tells Abram to go to a land 'that I will show you'. He promises him:
  - The land.
  - A great nation of his descendants.
  - A blessing and a great name.
  - That through him all the families of the earth shall be blessed (see Genesis 12:1–3).

- Abram and his wife Sara are old and childless. But God promises him that his offspring shall be as numerous as the stars in the heaven. 'And he believed the Lord, and he counted it to him as righteousness' (Genesis 15:1–6). These promises are formalised as a covenant, and Abram's name is changed to Abraham (father of a multitude – Genesis 17).

- Eventually the promise is fulfilled with the birth of Isaac; then Isaac fathers Jacob who, in turn, fathers twelve sons. A fairly detailed narrative leads to the situation where the entire family is resident in Egypt. In time, the king of Egypt enslaves the Hebrews (the descendants of Jacob) and puts them to forced labour (Genesis 21—50).

4 The exodus: a template of salvation

- The situation of the Hebrews becomes desperate. God appoints Moses to confront Pharaoh and to issue God's command to let his people go. It takes the ten plagues to convince Pharaoh to let them go, and even then he has second thoughts and pursues them. Having spared the faithful through the Passover lamb, God brings the nation out by a miracle in the Red Sea and destroys the pursuing armies of Egypt (Exodus 1—15). Let me remind you that the main character in this big story is God himself.

- The descendants of Abraham, Isaac and Jacob come to Mount Sinai and are now recognised as the nation of Israel. At Sinai, God gives the law through Moses: a body of instruction given to the Israelites concerning their life as the redeemed people of God (Exodus 20—23). God seals the covenant made with Israel with the blood of sacrifice (Exodus 24).

- Next, Israel receives the Lord's commands for a tabernacle and priesthood. God will dwell in their midst but only on his terms. His contact with the people will be mediated through the priestly ministry of the tabernacle (Exodus 25—40). Other laws are given to the people about life as the special people of God (Leviticus).

5 Entry into and possession of the promised land

- Unbelief leads to a false start in the process of taking possession of the land. A whole generation is condemned to die in the wilderness because they refused the command of God to go in and possess the land (Numbers). After 40 years in the desert, as the next generation prepares to enter, God speaks through Moses to prepare them for this momentous step (Deuteronomy).

- Under the leadership of Joshua, the Israelites cross the Jordan and begin to take possession of Canaan. The incursion is largely successful and the land is divided into tribal areas (Joshua). However, many enclaves of the idolatrous Canaanites, and others, are left. This leads to constant warfare and many challenges to the Israelites' possession of the land and to their faithfulness to God. God sends a series of judges to deal with the situation (Judges).

6 Consolidation, greatness and kingship

- In time, Samuel is established as prophet over Israel. The fledgling nation is beset by hostile neighbours such as the Philistines. The people begin to hanker for a king to rule over them 'like the nations'. Samuel presides over the choice of Saul, whose rule is abortive. Then a young David is chosen by God and anointed by Samuel. Saul continues to reign and sees David as a threat to his power. The death of Saul at the hands of the Philistines sees David anointed as king (1 Samuel).

- David's most notable achievements include the capture of the Jebusite city of Jerusalem and bringing the ark of the covenant to the city. He also achieves political greatness for the kingdom of Israel. Even though he commits murder and adultery, he is established as the king God has chosen (2 Samuel).

7 Decline, schism and exile

- When David dies, his son by Bathsheba, Solomon, becomes king. He rules over the greatest and most extensive kingdom of Israel ever. He is noted for the God-given gift of wisdom, and for the building of the temple. The glory did not last, as Solomon plays the fool with pagan women. On his death, his son Rehoboam continues the idolatrous decline. Led by Jeroboam, the ten northern tribes rebel and separate, setting up the kingdom of Israel. Judah and Benjamin remain in the south as the kingdom of Judah. Despite the apostasy within Judah, God keeps his promises to David and his dynasty survives for over 300 years. During that time there are evil kings and some good ones. Two of the most virtuous kings, Hezekiah and Josiah, attempt to reform the faith of Judah, but it is too little, too late (1 and 2 Kings).

- The northern kingdom remains apostate and falls to the powerful Assyrians in 722BC. Many of the population are taken into exile and foreigners brought in. The southern kingdom is able to survive the onslaught of the Assyrians but falls to the Babylonians in 597BC. In 586BC, Jerusalem and the temple are destroyed. On both occasions, many of the leading citizens are deported to Babylon (2 Kings).

- Most of the major and minor prophets were written around this period. They are mostly either God warning his people through the prophet that their present sinfulness will result in exile (such as Jeremiah), or comforting his people during exile and reminding them that he will not abandon them (such as the later parts of Isaiah).

8 Return and reconstruction

- When the Babylonian empire falls to the Persians, a new policy is adopted affecting captive peoples. Cyrus the king decrees in 538 BC that captives can return to their homelands. The books of Ezra and Nehemiah tell of the return and the beginnings of the reconstruction of Jerusalem and the temple. The people of Judah are still under the overall control of the Persians and remain so until the coming of Alexander the Great in the fourth century BC.

> The storyline of the New Testament continues the storyline of the Old Testament to make a complete narrative.

- Some of the minor prophets wrote in this period, encouraging God's people that God is still for them (such as Haggai and Malachi).

9 The Jews in the intertestamental period

- Alexander and his successors set out to Hellenise the lands of the Ancient Near East. Jewish religion and culture clashed with Hellenistic Greek culture in many ways and the Jews suffered much persecution. The Maccabean revolt in the second century did little to relieve this situation. Then the Romans came. The Jews thus had suffered captivity and oppressive rule since the end of the sixth century and in the time of Jesus we find them subservient to Rome.

10 Jesus and the founding of the Christian church

- The four Gospels tell their story from individual points of view; the same story but different aspects. Their subject is Jesus of Nazareth – his birth, life, death, resurrection and ascension. The Acts of the Apostles takes up the narrative from the ascension of Jesus (Acts is volume two of Luke's Gospel). The first part tells mainly of the early experiences of the Jewish church and the concern of these first Christians to understand where the Gentiles fit into the scheme of things. The second part is mainly about the mission of the Jews to the Gentiles and, in particular, the missionary journeys of Paul.

- The Epistles, mostly written by Paul, are written to deal with various situations in the fledgling churches which usually contain a mixture of Jews and Gentiles. Revelation (John's 'apocalypse') is an elaborate letter to persecuted churches in Asia Minor to encourage them with assurances of the victory of God and his Christ.

> The biblical narrative comes to its climax with the person of Jesus of Nazareth as the fulfiller of all the Old Testament promises.

This storyline is the medium through which the plan and purpose for salvation are revealed.

Summary of the storyline

Now let's put the main features of the storyline together. You will have noticed that the biblical narrative concentrates on, and is structured by, some key events involving God and his chosen people. God is the principal doer in all these events:

- Creation.
- The expulsion from Eden because of humankind's fall into sin.
- The covenant of salvation.

- The exodus as a template of salvation; the giving of the law.
- The entry into and possession of the promised land.
- The consolidation of the nation leading to kingship.
- Decline, schism and exile into Babylon.
- Return and reconstruction.
- The intertestamental period.
- Jesus and the founding of the Christian church.
- The new creation for the redeemed.

These are the events that we should be concentrating on. The mass of detail that emerges within the narratives belongs within this essential framework of the plan and purpose of God, which reaches its goal with Jesus. We must now look at the structure of this revelation in relation to the narrative. Remember, God is the principal character.

Key note
To get the 'big picture' you need to start with a timeline that focuses on the key persons and events that God uses to reveal the pattern of redemption.

Take a moment to reflect…

- Think about the idea that Old Testament history is the history of the acts of God.
- Read Acts 13:13–43. This is Paul's first recorded sermon. Notice how he preaches the gospel as the culmination of God's acts among his people Israel.
- What are the main events that Paul focuses on, and why do you think he does so?
- Can you suggest why Paul says that the Old Testament promises are fulfilled in the resurrection (vv. 32–33)?

Tip: Aim for the essential narrative first; you can fill in the details later.

4

The kingdom of God as a unifying theme

At first sight, the Bible may seem to be a large accumulation of largely unrelated pieces of literature. I have suggested an approach to this considerable collection of books that enables us to spot the structure and the patterns that give it its unity. So, what kind of unity is there?

The unity of the Bible

There are three main dimensions to the Bible that are of concern to us:

1 It is literature, a book, or rather a collection of 66 books, and we need to take account of the many ways writing was used to communicate. There is little by way of unity here other than the very general fact that writing was used to communicate God's word.
2 It has a historical storyline which I have outlined in the previous chapter. There is a unity in this, in that it deals with the history of the people of God. The overall narrative is coherent.
3 It has a message, a theological content, that speaks to us as God's word about his purpose to establish his kingdom. As literature, the Old Testament is no different from any other collection of writings. We need to reckon with the way language is used in its various parts. But, the Old Testament being what it is, we need to understand the historical context of

> The literary characteristics and the historical narrative both serve the theological message about salvation and the kingdom of God.

any text. And we need to try to understand what the theological content of every part of the Old Testament consists of.

The story that I have outlined in the previous chapter is continuous, despite it not being obvious from the outline that there is an overarching unity to the whole Bible. And, given the gap of about 400 years between the Old Testament story and the New Testament accounts of Jesus and the apostles, there may appear to be no obvious connection between the two. Until, that is, we investigate the attitude of Jesus and the New Testament writers to the Old Testament as the scriptures that point to Jesus and are fulfilled in and by him. It should become clear to the attentive reader that God progressively reveals his plan and purpose in the process of salvation history.

The literary dimension of the Bible is marked by diversity rather than obvious unity. Its unity lies in the storyline which has been outlined above. This points us to the historical dimension. First of all, when we examine the historical dimension, we see that there is a coherent storyline in the Old Testament from creation to the return of the Jews from the Babylonian exile. Second, we recognise that there are significant parts of the Old Testament that are not narratives. These include the songs of praise and thanksgiving, lamentations and wisdom. Most of the Psalms, Proverbs, the Song of Songs, and Ecclesiastes would come under this non-narrative material. Within the narratives, we find laws and regulations, genealogies, lists, parables and fables that are not by nature narrative. Then there is the considerable body of literature that consists of prophetic oracles which condemn unfaithfulness and idolatry, threaten judgement and predict a future when God will judge and save.

The non-narrative material belongs as expressions of Israel's faith. Although often contentious, many attempts have been made to identify the period and circumstances of Israel's history from which these literary expressions of faith come. It was once the normal scholarly practice to try to identify the texts behind the biblical texts;

that is, to isolate various earlier strands and to reconstruct their history. More recently there has been a welcome tendency to treat the individual works as the finished documents that we have, and to try to understand how they function in the Bible.

While the literary and historical dimensions must be taken into account, they are only the medium and the context of the theological message of the Bible. The unity of the Bible is only partially established on the basis of the coherence of the overall canon of scripture. The main reason for asserting the unity of the Bible is the witness of Jesus and the

> The literature and historical narratives in the Bible are the medium and context of the theological message.

New Testament writers themselves. When you remember that the New Testament was in the process of being written only after the events of Jesus' life, death and resurrection, you should be able to understand the fact that the only scriptures that Jesus and the apostles referred to was our Old Testament.

The shape of the historical timeline

In the following diagram I have drawn a representation of the history of God's people from creation to new creation. The horizontal lines represent the migration to Egypt of Jacob's family and then the Exodus, the separation of Judah and Israel, and the Babylonian exile and return. The idea is to give you, at a glance, a simple concept of the biblical story. Biblical history, especially that of the Old Testament does seem rather complicated when first encountered. I suggest that you concentrate on the big picture and fill in the details later as they come to hand in your reading. A few key dates are included.

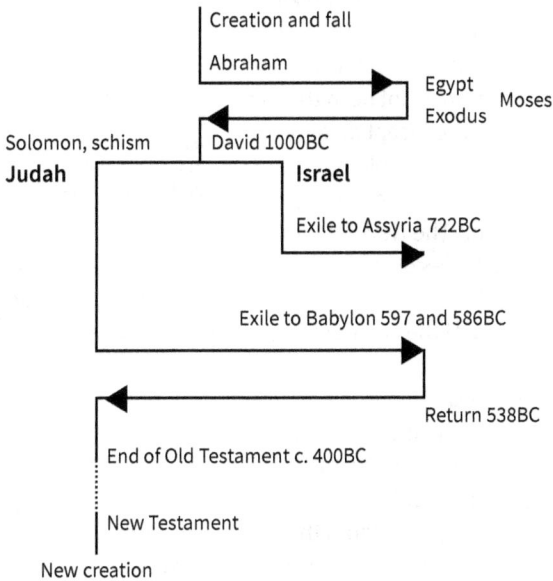

Diagram 2: The biblical timeline

A central theme of biblical revelation

There are more ways than one to conceive of the structure of the biblical revelation. This is because there are a number of significant themes that can be chosen as the basis for the way we make our analysis of the theological message of the Bible. When these are true to the biblical theology, they are complementary, not contradictory. So, for example, we can use the important central theme of the covenants that God makes with his people. If we do this, our analysis will be governed by the way the various covenants occur and are seen to relate to one another. Another central theme is the dwelling of God with his people, and the temple.

I favour using the theme of 'the kingdom of God'. This is not a term used in the Old Testament and some have criticised its use as a uniting theme because of that fact. However, the actual words may not be in the Old Testament but the concept certainly is. I want to suggest a simple and basic definition of what we mean by the kingdom of God.[7] The New Testament idea is that God rules over his people in a place he prepares for them. Thus, the kingdom of God is God's people in God's place under God's rule. The history of the kingdom and redemption goes like this:

> The kingdom of God is simply defined as
> God's people,
> in God's place,
> under God's rule.

- The kingdom is established in prototype in Eden.
- The kingdom is lost to humanity at the fall.
- The kingdom is promised to Abraham.
- The kingdom is lost in the captivity in Egypt.
- The entry into the kingdom through redemption is foreshadowed in the Exodus and Israel's entry into Canaan.
- The kingdom is patterned in the kingdoms of David and Solomon.
- The kingdom is lost in the exile to Babylon.
- The restoration of the kingdom is promised again by the prophets.
- The kingdom is proclaimed by Jesus and fulfilled by him.
- The kingdom is the promised inheritance of those who belong to Christ.
- The kingdom will be consummated when Jesus returns in glory.

The structure of kingdom revelation

A word about covenant and kingdom: the two are closely related. I favour concentrating on the latter as our guiding theme, since covenant is the formalising of the promises of God to bring in his kingdom. That is, the covenant is the vehicle or medium through which the promise of the kingdom is conveyed. We have to make a choice somewhere in trying to schematise the Bible in a way that is comprehensive and which does not distort the biblical evidence.

As a student, I was introduced to the idea of a comprehensive, simple, yet accurate summary of the Bible. God's kingdom and the way into it is revealed in three main stages:

1 It is revealed in Old Testament history, especially in the covenant with Abraham and the succeeding events leading up to the dedication of the temple by Solomon. The decline of Judah after Solomon highlights the factor of judgement.

2 When Solomon's kingdom goes into the decline that leads to the destruction of Jerusalem and the exile of the people into Babylon, the prophets take up the story. The latter prophets interpret the decline of Israel as God's judgement on their sin. At the same time, they promise that God will be faithful to his promises and will act to restore a redeemed people into his kingdom.

3 This restoration does not occur in Old Testament times. Then Jesus comes proclaiming that the kingdom of God is at hand. The New Testament announces the fulfilment of God's promises in Jesus.

This structure recognises that the basic ingredients of the kingdom of God, including how sinners can enter it, are stated progressively in Israel's history, are restated in the prophetic eschatology (view of the future) and are fulfilled in Christ. We can represent these three stages of revelation in a diagrammatic way. Diagrams, by their very nature, can represent only basic elements if they

> **The kingdom of God and salvation are revealed in three stages:**
> 1 Old Testament history
> 2 Prophetic eschatology
> 3 Fulfilment in Christ

are to be understandable to ordinary mortals, and if they are to avoid distorting the truth. Bear in mind, then, that the following three-stage diagrams can only suggest the main outline of progressive kingdom revelation. Notwithstanding the limitations, I strongly believe that something like these diagrams fulfil a very useful function in showing essential relationships within the main message of scripture.

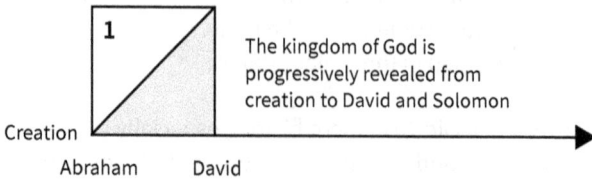

Diagram 3a: The first stage of redemptive revelation

In diagram 3a above, the biblical timeline runs from left to right at the base: creation leads to the persons of Abraham and David. Further revelation will progress from there. The square numbered 1 contains the shaded triangle formed by the diagonal line. This diagonal shows that revelation is progressive: in other words, Abraham knew more than Adam, and David knew more than Abraham. Thus, as the historical process advances, so does the revelation of salvation and the kingdom. The key points that will resurface later on, and especially in the New Testament, are:

- Creation (and the fall into sin).
- Judgement on the rebellious human race.
- God's move to redeem a sinful people for his kingdom.
  - The covenant with Abraham.
  - The captivity in Egypt and the redemptive work of God in the Exodus.
  - The law given as instructions to the redeemed people including the tabernacle.
  - The priesthood and sacrificial system.
  - The entry into the promised land and possession of it.
  - The establishment of the nation of Israel in its land.
- Kingship of David and Solomon.
- The city of Jerusalem as God's city.
- The temple.

So you can see that between God's calling of Abraham and the kingdom of David and Solomon, a lot has happened which reveals God's kingdom and how one can enter it.

At this point I want to introduce you to a technical term which is basic to understanding how the Old Testament can be read as a book about Christ. The word is 'typology' and with it a related word, 'type'. You should not be scared off by a couple of technical terms such as these. They are helpful for understanding the structure of the Bible. However, we should try to understand clearly how these terms can be used validly and how they have often been abused.

> Typology is a word we use to describe how a person, event or institution in the Old Testament foreshadows its fulfilment in the New Testament.

Typology is about the way that references to a person, an event or even an institution foreshadow a later use of these things in a way that corresponds with them but which is more significant. A type is such a person, event or institution that foreshadows a fulfilment, which is called the antitype. The exodus from Egypt, the sacrificial system and the temple are all examples of types that foreshadow Christ as the antitype. Ideas such as 'shadow and solid reality', 'promise and fulfilment' or 'symbol and meaning' all relate to the idea of typology. Diagram 3a represents those people, events and institutions that occur in the biblical history up the time of the height of the kingdoms of David and Solomon. Every one of these is taken up somewhere in the prophetic oracles but projected into a future and glorious kingdom. Then the historical and the prophetic elements are fulfilled in the person and work of Jesus Christ.

A word of warning: typology is not a matter of mere association of ideas or of free association. The type must point to the actual theology that foreshadows the theology of the antitype, that is, of the person, event or institution that it looks forward to. The theological significance of the type must correspond in some significant way to the theology of the antitype. Typology becomes spurious when the theological correspondence is not there. So, for example, the sheep gate in Nehemiah's Jerusalem does not foreshadow the fact that Jesus is the good shepherd. Nor do the pomegranate decorations on the priest's robes point us to the fruit of the Spirit. There is a big difference between biblical typology and fanciful allegorising. We will come back to this subject as we progress.

Let us now look at the second stage of biblical revelation.

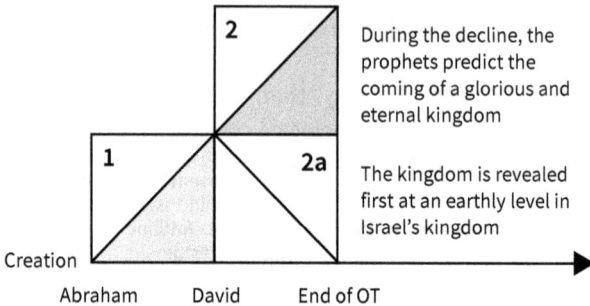

During the decline, the prophets predict the coming of a glorious and eternal kingdom

The kingdom is revealed first at an earthly level in Israel's kingdom

Diagram 3b: The prophetic view of the future kingdom

Following the timeline at the base from David (and Solomon) to the end of the Old Testament, the diagonal line descending in square 2a indicates the decline of the kingdom. During this period, the prophetic revelation comes into play. You will notice that I have drawn the second stage exactly the same shape as the first but placed it at a higher level. This indicates that what the prophets predict, as they contemplate the destruction of the earthly kingdom of David and Solomon, is a renewal of the kingdom along the same lines but with an important difference. When it comes, it will be perfect, eternal and glorious. This difference is represented by the darker shading and elevation. It should be clear that the prophetic revelation is necessary because, although the historical kingdom revealed the pattern of salvation and the kingdom of God, it was not itself the glorious reality that is yet to come.

The shape of this prophetic view of the coming kingdom is thus based on the shape of the past historical kingdom in which God revealed the essential dimensions of his kingdom and the way into it. This suggests that, if the historic kingdom is a type of the true kingdom to come, the collective oracles of the prophets confirm this structure, or shape, of the kingdom and redemption. In Old Testament times this kingdom, variously described and foretold by the prophets, never eventuates. The return from Babylon might seem to be leading to this kingdom but, however much the situation of the Jews improves, the reconstructed Judah is *not* the kingdom of God. Only when we come to the New Testament and the claims of Jesus do we have the real fulfilment.

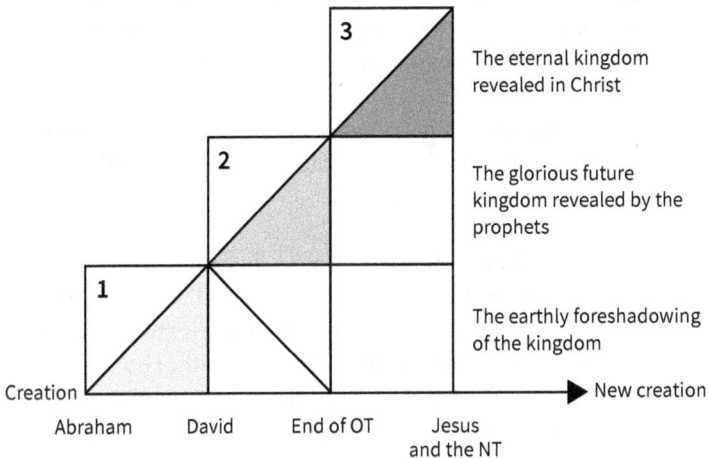

Diagram 3c: The fulfilment of the kingdom in Christ

The three diagrams (3a, b and c) are intended to represent the three stages of kingdom revelation that span the whole Bible. Diagram 3a lays down the basis for a biblical typology. In Diagram 3b we represent the eschatology of the prophets as confirming the historical typology. The fulfilment or antitype is shown in Diagram 3c as the person and work of Jesus Christ.

A further word about typology

When we look at the idea of the typology of the Bible from the other end – that is, starting with Jesus in his gospel – the question arises: 'What exactly does Jesus fulfil from the Old Testament?' Some possible or tentative answers to this question might be:

- He fulfils mainly those Old Testament texts that are quoted in the New Testament as applying to him. For example, Isaiah 7:14: 'Behold, the virgin shall conceive and bear a son, and shall call his name Immanuel.' This is cited in Matthew 1:23. Or Hosea 11:1: 'Out of Egypt I called my son' cited in Matthew 2:15.
- He fulfils the basic structure of salvation that unfolds in the history of Israel, but leaves a lot of Old Testament detail as irrelevant.
- He fulfils everything included in the restoration of the whole creation, in the new heavens and the new earth.

Clearly there are some differences of approach in these examples. If we want to uncover the Christological fulfilment of the Old Testament, how far can we go?

There are two distinct, though related, questions here. We can propose answers to the question, 'What is fulfilled?' and that is probably the first step we need to take. But there is still the practical question of 'How is it fulfilled?' to be dealt with. Looking at the matter of the overall role of Jesus, we can question Paul and his statement in Ephesians 1:3–10. Briefly stated, Paul blesses God for our salvation (vv. 3–8) which he places in the wider context of God's purpose in 'the fullness of time, to unite all things in [Christ], things in heaven and things on earth'. I want to suggest that Paul's reference to the fullness of time (compare Galatians 4:4) refers to what happened at the incarnation (the 'becoming flesh' of God). This will be consummated universally at the return of Christ, but it happened when God the Son became a human being in union with his full deity. What happened in the first coming of Christ will happen again, but in a different way, when he returns.

A great deal hangs here on who and what we believe Jesus was and is. If you have made the decision to limit Jesus to being the most perfect human being that has ever lived (or even less than that), your take on his 'uniting all things' will be extremely limited by what you think he was. If you accept the orthodox teaching of the Christian church that Jesus was, and still is, truly human and truly divine, then you will be more accepting of the proposal

> **Two questions need to be answered:**
> 1 What does Jesus fulfil?
> 2 How does Jesus fulfil?

I want to make here. This is not the place for a discussion about Jesus being God and man. I believe the Bible teaches that doctrine and the Christian church has acknowledged it from the beginning.

The biblical doctrine of creation tells us that humanity was made as the pinnacle of creation and, in that sense, embodies all creation. That Adam was formed from the dust and will return to the dust (Genesis 3:19) is a reminder of that. Thus, the fall of humanity meant the fall of creation; the redemption of humanity will mean the redemption of creation (Romans 8:18–23). Given that Jesus was true God and true human being, we have in his historic person a vital union between all dimensions of reality: God, humanity and (non-human) creation. This union is not a merging into an undifferentiated reality but the restoration of the proper relationships between God, humanity and creation. If Jesus truly is God, man and creation, he did unite all things in himself at his first coming.

Once we accept that the redemptive work of Jesus is all-embracing, the implications for the Bible are enormous. If you think Jesus came to save only our 'souls', then what do you expect is the future of our bodies? The human, bodily life of Jesus, his bodily death and resurrection and his bodily ascension mean he saves our whole persons: body, mind and soul. And he redeems the creation. That is why the scriptures refer to the new heavens and the new earth in the consummation (Isaiah 65:17; Revelation 21:1). Believers are not destined to inhabit a vague and formless spirit world. We look for the resurrection of the body and everlasting life in the new earth.

Jesus rebuked certain of the Jews for their unbelief thus:

> There is one who accuses you: Moses, on whom you have set your hope. If you believed Moses, you would believe me; for he wrote of me.
>
> JOHN 5:45–46

He did not thereby imply that Moses wrote about others as well. The texts we have looked at already indicate that Jesus saw the content of the Old Testament as being about him. And if there are parts of the Old Testament that are not about him, who or what can they be about? This is a serious question. If Jesus unites within himself all of reality (God, humanity and non-human creation), it does not leave much room for other things to be excluded from the equation.

To summarise:

- When humankind rebelled, God judged the whole creation.
- His plan of redemption is revealed in Old Testament history along with the prophetic word.
- His plan is implemented by restoring the relationships of reality representatively in Christ, by whose death he also deals with the problem of sin.
- Through the proclamation of the gospel, God restores all things in a process that will be consummated at the return of Christ.

Since Jesus is, in himself, 'God – man – world', everything that is either God, human or created has its meaning in Jesus and is related to him in some way. That, I believe, is the crux of the matter. Since Jesus is the God-Man, there is nothing that is not related to him in some way. It means that Jesus, in his person and work, provides the meaning of every fact in the universe. We acknowledge this when we recognise that his return in glory will bring about the consummation of all things and the final revelation of the kingdom of God. If everything is summed up in Christ, this must include the Old Testament.

Key note
The storyline of the Bible receives its unity mainly from the theological meaning contained in the acts of God and his progressive revelation of the kingdom of God and of the way of redemption.

Take a moment to reflect…

- Take time to reflect on the biblical teaching of Christ as the fulfiller of the Old Testament promises.
- Read Acts 2:14–36. This is Peter's Pentecost sermon. What does he say about the way the Old Testament is being fulfilled?
- Have you ever thought about the idea of a central theme for the whole Bible?

Tip: Try to develop the idea that the Bible is a book about God before it is about us. Think of the Bible as the one word of the one God about the one way of salvation through the one Saviour, Jesus Christ.

5

The shape of progressive revelation

By now you will have noticed that the movement through the history of salvation involves development or change in the way the truths of God's plan are revealed. We refer to this as *progressive revelation*. The progressiveness is seen in three ways:

- First, there is an unfolding over a period of time of the plan of God for salvation. Thus, for example, David knew more of the plan than Moses; Moses knew more than Abraham; and Abraham knew more than Noah.

  > Redemptive history means that revelation follows the historical process and is thus progressive.

- Second, a pattern of redemption is established, which is repeated by the prophets, but with a difference. Building on the now-fading historical kingdom revelation, the prophets project the future resulting from the faithfulness and sovereign purpose of God.
- Third, the pattern is fulfilled in Christ. This was not always appreciated by the disciples, who had built up a number of expectations that somehow did not fit with how Jesus revealed himself and his ministry.

Thus we have three successive stages in this progressive revelation:

1 The history of God's acts in the Old Testament narrative.
2 The prophets' perspective on the future fulfilment of God's plans.
3 The fulfilment of God's promises in the person and work of Christ.

We must look at these in a little more detail.

The progression of revelation

The Old Testament story presents us with a great multitude of characters and events. Again, I would emphasise the need initially to avoid being bogged down in the details. Try to grasp the main events and their significance. The same goes for the significant people and institutions. You can spend the rest of your life filling in the details. I do not want in any way to belittle the details, especially when you are engaged in a close reading in order to teach or preach from a confined part of the text. Nevertheless, there are certain key events and people that figure prominently in the whole process, and we can often spot these from the way they are repeatedly referred to and reflected on in the various texts of both the Old and New Testaments.

Old Testament redemptive history easily resolves itself into major ideas that are central to the theological message of the Bible. The key elements of the story of redemption can be summarised thus:

- Creation (then the fall and the progress of evil).
- Covenant.
- Captivity and exodus redemption.
- Entry into and possession of the land.
- Davidic king.
- Jerusalem (Zion).
- Temple.

> Old Testament redemptive history easily resolves itself into major ideas that are central to the message of the Bible.

The tragic side of the story is that, after the dedication of Solomon's temple, there is a steady decline leading to destruction and the exile into Babylon. This, say the prophets, is due to the idolatry and the unfaithfulness of the people of God. But the prophets also hold out the promise of God's absolute faithfulness and the prospect of his future action to save a faithful remnant of Israel and to bring in his kingdom. Now, compare the historical pattern (above) with the picture that the prophets build of this future saving act of God:

- New creation.
- New covenant.
- New captivity and exodus redemption.
- New entry and new possession of the land.
- New Davidic king.
- New Jerusalem.
- New temple.

The prophets don't set it out as neatly as I have because they are responding to different specific circumstances in the life of God's people. We have to build up this perspective from among

> The prophets' view of future salvation and the kingdom of God is a replay of the past historic revelation.

the 16 Old Testament prophetic books, each of which contributes something to a future hope. The overall picture that they build shows that their God-inspired view of the future fulfilment of all God's promises is a kind of replay or recapitulation of the past historical events in God's revelation. But, although the pattern is the same, there is one big difference. Unlike the failed kingdom of Israel's history, the future kingdom will be perfect, glorious and eternal.

The table below gives you some representative texts in the prophetic books that speak of the future in terms that recall the past history of Israel.

Israel's history	Prophetic future	Some prophetic texts
Creation	New creation	Isaiah 65:17
Covenant	New covenant	Jeremiah 31:31–34; Ezekiel 34:25–31; 36:24–28
Exodus	New exodus	Isaiah 40:1–5; 43:1–7, 15–21; 48:20–21; 49:24–26; 51:9–11; Jeremiah 23:7–8

Israel's history	Prophetic future	Some prophetic texts
Entry and possession of the land	New entry and new possession of the land	Isaiah 32:14–20; 35:1–10; Jeremiah 23:7–8; 29:10–14; Ezekiel 34:11–16
Jerusalem	New Jerusalem	Isaiah 44:24–28; 46:13; 49:14–21; 51:3
Temple	New temple	Isaiah 2:2–3; Ezekiel 40—47; Zechariah 4:6–9
Davidic king	New David	Isaiah 9:2–7; 11:1–5; 16:5; 55:3–5; Jeremiah 23:1–6; Ezekiel 34:20–24; 37:24–28; Amos 9:11

Table 1: The prophetic recapitulation of the historic past

Fulfilment in Christ

The New Testament constantly refers, either explicitly or implicitly, to Christ as the fulfiller of the promises, prophecies and expectations of the Old Testament. The progression within the Old Testament of Israel's earthly and historical experience of God's acts and revelation continues in the New Testament. What the people of God experienced in the history of the covenant of redemption was repeated by the prophets, but envisioned at a higher level. This prophetic vision does not find fulfilment in Old Testament times. In the New Testament, the progression is to the fulfilment in Christ. That means that our principle for interpreting the Old Testament must be drawn from the New Testament; it is a principle of Christological fulfilment. We must allow the New Testament to dictate our understanding of what fulfilment involves.

There is one popular alternative to the Christological fulfilment that sounds reasonable, indeed self-evident. It asserts that fulfilment must be literal. In other words, the fulfilment must correspond exactly and literally to the promises. The idea is 'God says what he means and means what he says.' Of course! But that does not mean that literalistic fulfilment follows. I do not believe the New Testament supports such literalism, and if it doesn't, then we shouldn't either.

We need to understand that fulfilment in Christ means that some of the outward aspects of the historic and prophetic stages become absorbed into the reality which is Christ. This is because the *theological significance* of institutions, such as the temple and the promised land, is found in Christ. It is in the nature of type-antitype, of shadow-substance or of promise-fulfilment that there is difference between the former and the latter. Thus, in the Old Testament, the land, the city of Jerusalem and the temple form concentric circles enclosing the idea of God dwelling with his people. That is why Jesus (*Immanuel* – God with us) fulfils the function of all three. While Jesus declares himself to be the new temple (John 2:19–21), we find that the land, city and temple all recede from view in the theology of the New Testament. They will re-emerge in the apocalyptic Old Testament language of the book of Revelation, describing the consummation of the promises at the return of Christ as the New Eden and the New Jerusalem. But note that in Revelation 21, the temple drops out of sight altogether because God is actually with his people. There is no longer a need for the symbolic representation of his presence. That is why there was no temple in Eden and there will be none in the New Jerusalem (Revelation 21:22–24).

If the literalist interpreters were correct, we would expect the New Testament to be eloquent in pointing us to the literalistic fulfilments. But the eschatology of the New Testament is strangely silent about the very things that literalism says must come to pass.

Israel's history	Prophetic future	Fulfilment in Christ
Creation	New creation	New creation in Christ
Covenant	New covenant	New covenant
Exodus	New exodus	Christ achieves the true exodus

Israel's history	Prophetic future	Fulfilment in Christ
Entry into and possession of the land	New entry and possession of new land	Jesus is God dwelling with his people
Jerusalem	New Jerusalem	Christ now the focal point of God with his people
Temple	New temple	Jesus is the new temple
Davidic king	New David	Jesus, son of David

Table 2: The pattern of revelation fulfilled in Christ

The 'now' and the 'not yet'

The New Testament has a unique way of talking about the relationship the Christian believer has to Jesus, to his saving work and to the final outcome of it. The Old Testament prophets looked forward to a day when God would act finally and definitively to bring salvation to his people and show his rule over all. In some of the prophets, this day was referred to as 'the day of the Lord'. Although there is no indication of the duration of the actual 'day', the Old Testament believer could be excused for thinking that the events would all happen at once, in one final act of God. That is probably why the disciples of Jesus took quite a while to get their heads around the fact that the Messiah should suffer first, and why the kingdom of God did not appear in its ultimate glory with the first coming of Jesus.

> The gospel is the work of Christ *for* us, 2,000 years ago in Palestine.
>
> The fruit of the gospel (growing as a Christian) is the work of Christ *in* us through his word and Spirit.

The disciples of Jesus had to cope with the fact that he came doing signs and wonders, but was cruelly put to death by the people he came amongst: his own people (John 1:11). So, Jesus comes. He goes away. But he has also promised that he will come again. Some of the seeming ambiguities in the Old Testament are thus ironed out as the New Testament authors reflect on the significance of the two comings of Christ and of the coming of the Spirit of Christ in between. The perspective that is very clear in the New Testament, especially in the epistles, is that there are three aspects to the saving work of God in Christ:

1 Jesus of Nazareth came to do *for* us what we could not do for ourselves in his life, death and resurrection.
2 The risen Christ sends his Spirit on to his church to enable the preaching of the gospel and to turn people in faith to himself. The Spirit of Christ does his work *in* us to convert and sanctify us.
3 Christ will one day return personally and in glory to judge the living and the dead. He will bring in his glorious kingdom *with* us in the consummation of all his promises and saving work.

All three of these aspects constitute the fulfilment and consummation of all the promises and prophecies in the Old Testament. It is important that we distinguish the work that Christ did *for* us at his first coming from the work his Spirit does *in* us in our daily Christian lives. The proclamation of the gospel is concerned with the '*for* us' work of Christ, which is finished and perfect. The fruit of the gospel, its effects in our lives, is the work of the Spirit *in* us as he applies the word of scripture to us. This work, the subject of sermons and studies on the Christian life, is not finished and not yet perfect.

Now let's be practical! We cannot add to or subtract from the finished work of Christ *for* us. And, since it was perfect, anything we try to add to it would only confuse our understanding of the gospel. We can either embrace it by faith, or reject it in unbelief. If we believe it and put our trust and confidence in the promise of salvation for those who believe, we are made God's children through grace and adoption. God attributes to us the righteousness of Christ and we are justified by his grace. We cannot add to our acceptance with God, nor can we subtract from it, since it is based on the acceptance that the Father showed Jesus when he raised him from the dead and took him to his presence in heaven.

How this affects Christian living

Remember the prophets projected various perspectives on the day of the Lord, the day when God would act finally and definitively to bring in his kingdom. This would involve two things: the final judgement and destruction of the enemies of God, and the final salvation of the redeemed people of God. But the prophets did not really tell us any more than that it would happen on a day when the Lord comes to judge and conclude the present age, and to inaugurate the new age for ever. The general pattern could be represented as in the following diagram:

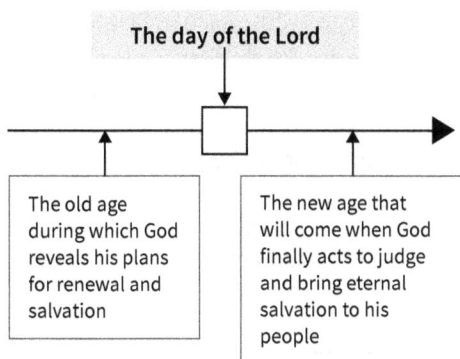

Diagram 4a: The Old Testament prophetic view of the two ages

The pattern in the Old Testament appears to be that the old age will come to an end on the 'day of the Lord' and the new age will then be inaugurated. We have seen how the promises of this day, which would lead to final salvation, judgement and the new age, are not fulfilled during the period of the Old Testament. When Jesus begins his ministry he declares the kingdom of God to be at hand. Now here's our problem:

- Jesus comes and proclaims the kingdom has come. Then he lives, suffers, dies, rises and ascends to the Father.

- Despite all this, things go on in the world pretty much as they always have. There is no obviously visible new age, only the church and its gospel message about the means to enter the new age on the basis of the death and resurrection of Jesus.
- Even though Jesus has come, the New Testament points us in three directions: the first is back to the gospel event (Jesus); the second is to our present life in Christ; and the third is forward to the future return of Christ and the consummation of his kingdom.

Remember the distinction between the *for* us, *in* us and *with* us work of God. It can be simply resolved by recognising that the New Testament makes clear what is not so clear in the Old Testament. The New Testament shows us the overlap of the two ages. Although the new age has broken in with the first coming of Jesus to save, the old age continues. When Jesus returns in glory to judge the living and the dead, the old age finally will be wound up. We can represent this pattern of 'now' and 'not yet' by the diagram 4b below.

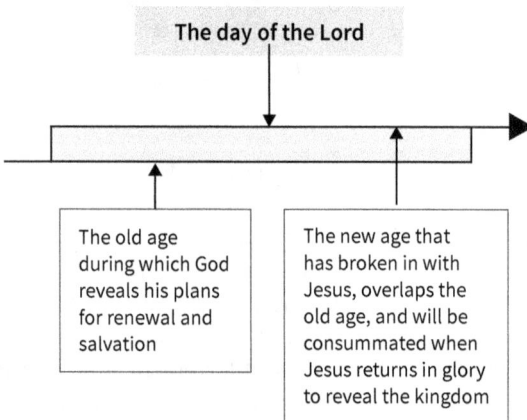

Diagram 4b: The New Testament view of the overlap of the two ages

From this you will observe that the Old Testament's day of the Lord is fulfilled in the period between the first coming of Jesus and his return at the end of the age. In diagram 4c below, the overlap of the ages is represented in New Testament terms.

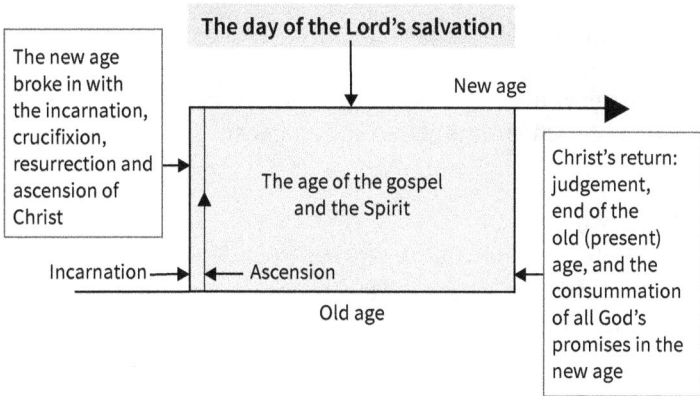

Diagram 4c: The New Testament view of the two ages

This overlap of the ages results from the nature of Christ's coming, and must be taken into account when we want to trace the New Testament fulfilment of the Old Testament promises.

Let me remind you again of the three distinct, though intimately related ways that the fulfilment takes place:

- First, there is the once-for-all fulfilment in the person and work of Jesus: he is all these things *for* us.
- Second, there is the fulfilment that goes on happening *in* the world and *in* us who are united to Christ by faith. This is done by the word (Bible) and the Spirit.
- Third, there is the fulfilment in the universal consummation of all God's purposes which will take place *with* us, when Christ returns.

Also note that nothing happens in the *in* us and *with* us fulfilments that has not happened already in the gospel *for* us event at Christ's first coming: these will simply happen in a different way:

- God did it all for us representatively and effectually in Christ.
- God goes on doing it in us and the world through the power of God's Spirit in the preaching of the gospel.
- God will do it finally, universally, consummately and eternally when Christ returns in glory.

We must now turn to consider the practical application of these principles to actual parts of the Old Testament.

Key note
The revelation of the kingdom of God, and of the way into it, is given in three stages: the history of God's deeds in the Old Testament, the prophetic view of the future deeds of God, and the fulfilment of all this in Jesus Christ.

Take a moment to reflect...

- Take a look at some of the Bible references in table 1 and become more familiar with the way the prophets see a future fulfilment of God's saving acts of the past.
- Read Colossians 3:1–5. Notice the involvement of the Christian in the past events of Christ's work, the present implications for our Christian lives and the future hope for Christ's return.
- How does the day of the Lord provide the assurance that God is in control of world history?

Tip: Try to get into the habit of seeing the progressiveness of God's revelation and realise that this means that not every part of the Bible has the same relationship to Jesus or to us.

Part 2

Working with the texts

6

Some key events in biblical revelation

A proposed method of approach

In the light of what I have suggested regarding the main dimensions and structure of the Bible, we can propose an approach that takes account of these elements. Treating the literary dimension is never purely a literary pursuit. Exegesis starts with the literature within our chosen text, but every portion of text, even whole books, must be seen within the context of the wider narrative. This applies even when our chosen text is

> The three dimensions of scripture – the literary, the historical and the theological – are closely related to one another.

not narrative. In other words, the three dimensions – literature, history and theology – are interdependent; they affect each other. The more you understand of the contents, structure and meaning of the Bible, the more you will be thinking of all three dimensions in relationship to each other. Let us now consider these three dimensions in turn.

1 Valuing the literary expression: exegesis

Exegesis involves getting out of a text what is actually in it. We look for the meaning that the text sets out to communicate. (*Eisegesis* is the reverse: reading into a text something that isn't there.) When we approach the text, a number of questions need to be considered, some of which we may answer instinctively and others we probably need to be reminded of.

- What is the meaningful unit of text? This might be a whole prophetic oracle, a parable, a complete event in narrative and so on. Here we recognise that we can easily distort texts by ignoring their context. The smaller the text we select, the greater the possibility of distorting its true meaning. Ascertaining the meaningful unit means we do not try to read a part of the unit out of context.

- What does this text actually say? How does the author use language to convey meaning, and what meaning is in this text? Here we recognise the place of various kinds of literary expression such as narration, metaphor, simile, poetic imagery and so on. We are concerned with the immediate meaning; application comes later.

- What does this text mean within its own immediate context? Put yourself in the place of the original author or reader: how would they have understood this text? How is the narrative structured and developed?

- How does the text function in the larger context? This might be the whole book, and it certainly involves its place in the finished canon of scripture. It is important to recognise that the objects of our concern are the finished books that the church has received as holy scripture. Some books may have developed from earlier manuscripts. As interesting as this may be, it is not our primary concern.

2 Understanding the historical context

- What kind of narrative is it? Does it select the details to emphasise a particular aspect of revelation? It may be stylised to achieve this. We should not expect ancient historians to be bound by modern rules of history writing.

- If this is narrative, how does it fit in with the wider story? Don't forget that the wider story involves the timeline from creation to the new creation. Generally, this is not a problem, but there are some passages that are not entirely clear as to where they fit.

- If this is not narrative, how does it fit in with the historical progression of the wider narrative? Where, for example, would you place some of the non-narrative materials such as wisdom sayings or certain psalms? And how would an understanding of the historical context affect our grasp of the meaning of such a text?

3 Understanding the theological significance

- Theology is a word that simply means 'knowledge of God'. Bearing in mind that the Bible is about God, his plans and his doings, what does this text tell us about God?

- How does the theology of this passage relate to the wider context? You will find that this question becomes easier to answer the more you become familiar with the bigger picture of biblical revelation. This is because the Bible is both large and complex, but it is also a unity. Every part bears some relationship to every other part.

- How does the theology of this passage testify to Christ? A lot of people will ask first: 'What does this passage say about us?' This is to jump the gun. All that I have tried to explain in the first part of this study becomes relevant to this issue.

You will observe that these comments really overlap all the time. We are considering literature, historical context and theological meaning all the time. It is really not as straightforward as performing three successive tasks, but of perceiving the interaction of all three.

Thematic studies

One way of finding important links between the Old and New Testaments is to engage in thematic studies. I have already suggested the kingdom of God as a central theme that gives the scriptures their unity. But the kingdom contains many sub-themes that need to be identified. In what follows I want to suggest a number of very significant themes that are quite readily traced through the three stages of kingdom revelation that I have outlined.

Creation

There will be some who follow the 'creationist' line of asserting that Genesis 1 must be taken as literal historic narrative. I do not propose to argue for or against this position. Others will be content to accept that there is evidence of a schematised narration, which is not intended to give such a literalistic or strictly scientific meaning. You will have to decide for yourself which end of the spectrum you lean towards. Differences of opinion occur at the literary level: we need to decide what kind of literature the creation narratives are. I see the first account as a crafted and unique literary structure that points to the sovereign work of God, creating by his word all things out of nothing. Comparing the two accounts of creation (Genesis 1:1–2:3 and 2:4–25), we can see the different perspectives and purposes within them. There are several essential aspects to understanding what the Bible conveys by its teaching on creation.

- God creates everything out of nothing by his word. He establishes the rule of humanity over the rest of creation. He also defines the relationship of human beings to God and to the created order.
- The 'fall' is the result of the human rejection of God's rule. Adam and Eve are expelled from Eden and creation is made to fall with humanity. There is a certain element of 'un-creation' in this.
- The promise of a new creation is hinted at in Genesis 3:15. It begins to take on real shape with the covenant promises made to Abraham and his descendants through Isaac and Jacob.

- Further hints of a new creation occur in the related themes of the promise of a land, the redemption from the captivity in a foreign land and the final entry into the promised land of Canaan.
- When the apostasy of the Israelites leads finally to their removal from the promised land and to the exile into Babylon, the prophets have various ways of pointing to a future new creation. This will involve a renewal of the heavens and the earth, of the land, of the city and the temple, and the regeneration of a faithful remnant of God's people.
- Jesus comes and is, in himself, the new creation.
- Believers become part of the new creation by incorporation into Christ through faith.
- At Christ's return, the whole universe is involved: a new heaven and a new earth.

The covenant

A covenant is the promises God makes to his chosen people. It is based on the gracious purpose of God to have a people in his kingdom for ever. The rebellion of humanity against God will not be allowed to thwart this overarching purpose of God. The covenant is the formalising of this purpose in a way that specifies the promises of God and obligates the recipients to receive the benefits of the promises. There is a unilateral and unconditional aspect: God does not have a conference with the people in order to work out the details. He tells them what his plan is. There is also the bilateral and conditional aspect: the requirement for faithful obedience.

> The covenant is a central theme that structures the redemptive history of the Bible.

In the Bible, there are a number of distinct expressions of the covenant. They all link to the plan of God for his people. So, while there are several covenant expressions, they all contribute to the unity of the one plan of God.

- Some regard the very act of creation as covenantal. It becomes clear that God did not intend human rebellion to frustrate his plans for the whole of creation. God has committed himself to his creation.
- The first explicit reference to covenant is God's promise to Noah never to destroy the earth again by a flood in Genesis 9:8–17.
- The covenant of redemption begins to take shape in the promises of God to Abram in Genesis 12:1–3; 15:4–6, 18; 17:1–8. The essence of this covenant is the promise of:
  - A nation of descendants to be the people of God.
  - A land to live in before God.
  - Blessing through them to all the nations of the earth.
- This covenant is the basis of the acts of God for Israel:
  - The exodus as redemption from captivity in Egypt.
  - The instructions for the redeemed life in the Sinai law.
  - The entry into, and possession of, the promised land.
  - The chosen and anointed kinship of David.
  - The city of Jerusalem (Zion) as the focus of the land.
  - The temple as the focus of the dwelling of God among his people.
- Israel's disobedience and idolatry lead to the destruction of Jerusalem, the temple and the people as God's people in his land. But the prophets predict a renewed covenant of redemption.
- Jesus comes proclaiming 'the new covenant in my blood'.

The exodus

The exodus from Egypt is the main Old Testament revelation of the way of redemption, and the need for it. The chosen people of God are nevertheless sinful and must find redemption if they are to enjoy the blessings of the covenant. The salvation of God's people is accompanied by, and achieved along with, the judgement on the enemies of God. While the exodus from Egypt conveys a pattern of redemption, it quickly becomes evident that it only patterns and foreshadows the real redemption to come.

> The exodus was a necessary redemptive event based on the covenant promises to Abraham.

- The covenant with Abraham is the reason for the exodus from Egypt.
- The exodus is the necessary redemptive prelude to the attaining of the blessings of the covenant.
- The people of God in exile in Babylon are promised a second exodus.
- The return from Babylon does not deliver the prophesied benefits.
- Jesus comes to effect the true exodus from slavery to sin, Satan and death.

The tabernacle and sacrifice

After the exodus from Egypt, God gave instruction for the construction of the tabernacle to show that he dwelled with his people (Exodus 25:1–9). This presence of God is mediated through the prophetic word and the priestly ministry of sacrifice. This is necessary because they were sinful and could not come into God's presence. The presence of God was represented by the most holy place (the Holy of Holies) in which the ark of the covenant and the mercy seat were located. Only the high priest could enter, and that only once a year with the blood of sacrifice. This day of atonement described in Leviticus 16, along with all the other sacrifices, demonstrated the separation between God and human beings because of sin.

- Sacrifice to God goes back to the beginning of biblical history.
- The prescription for the tabernacle and sacrifices in the law of Moses gives context and meaning to the demand for such ritual. The tabernacle is portable to accommodate the unsettled nation.
- The sanctuary at Shiloh figures in the narrative of Samuel.
- Once the nation is settled in the promised land and David is anointed as God's choice of king, the matter of a permanent sanctuary arises.

> The tabernacle, and then the temple, were focal points that spoke of God dwelling with his people, and of the sacrifices needed to reconcile people to God.

- David is told he will not build the temple; his son will.
- Solomon's building and dedication of the temple mark the high point in Israel's history.
- When the temple is destroyed by the Babylonians, there is already in place a line of prophetic words about a rebuilding of a glorified temple. The rebuilt temple under Ezra and Nehemiah is a big disappointment.
- Jesus declares that he is the new temple and the true sacrifice for sin.
- Christians are built in this temple 'as living stones'.
- As there was no temple in Eden (God was really there in fellowship with his people) so there will be no temple in the new Jerusalem.

The promised land

If you remember that the situation of the covenanted people is one of exile from Eden, the promised land fits more easily into place. I have suggested that the basic idea of the kingdom of God is God's people living in the place God provides for them under his rule. When Adam and Eve were expelled from Eden, there is a real sense in which they become homeless. The land promised to Abraham and his descendants is an echo of Eden. When Israel enters the land of Canaan under Joshua, the situation develops so that the focus is on God dwelling with his people. The focus of the land becomes the city of God, and the focus of city becomes the temple as the dwelling place of God.

- Eden is the original land where God dwells with his people.
- Canaan is promised to Abraham and possessed by Joshua and the people.

> The promised land speaks of the place God is preparing for his people where they will dwell with him.

- The land is lost because of rebellion and the people expelled from the land in the Babylonian exile.
- The prophets promise a return of a faithful remnant of the people to the new land, which is to be a new Eden. The return from Babylon does not result in the fulfilment of this ideal.

- Jesus comes as Immanuel ('God with us') and thus fulfils in his person the function of the new land. He also goes away 'to prepare a place for you'.
- The actual land drops out of sight once Jesus fulfils its meaning. The book of Revelation reintroduces Old Testament imagery to describe the dwelling of God with his people on the new earth.

The Davidic kingship, Jerusalem and the temple

Kingship must not be confined to the place where the title 'king' is used. Adam and Eve were given dominion over the rest of the creation. This rule reflected the rule of God. In time, as the various pieces of the picture are assembled in the promised land, kingship emerges as a central expression of God's rule over his people. The anointing of the house of David establishes one line that will carry this rule of God, often only in name. When the Son of David appears he, Jesus, is shown by his works, his resurrection and ascension to be God's king over his people.

- Adam and Eve are the first rulers in the world.
- Under the covenant of redemption, various figures emerge as mediators of God's rule. Initially, it is the prophets such as Moses and Samuel who carry this role.
- Kingship is established in the house of David.
- The dynasty of David fails in the task and the throne is cut off in the Babylonian exile.
- The prophets promise a new King David as God's shepherd over his people.
- Jesus, as Son of David, is declared to be that king.

These few examples review some of the obvious Old Testament themes that point us to Christ. In fact, the unity of the Bible and the connectedness of all its parts together indicate that there is really no limit to the themes we can examine. Not all are as central to the message of the Bible as others. Nevertheless, as we study the Bible, we can always be on the lookout for themes that lead us to Christ. It is time now for us to consider some of the actual textual material in the Old Testament. By now, I trust, you will be developing your own sense of the nature of the Bible's unity and the centrality to it of the person and work of Jesus Christ.

Key note
Biblical revelation contains a number of major themes that relate to one another in a coherent way, and that establish the theology of the Old Testament, which foreshadows the person and work of Jesus Christ and prepares us for his coming.

Take a moment to reflect…

- Read John 8:48–59. What is Jesus getting at when he says, 'Abraham rejoiced that he would see my day. He saw it and was glad'?
- Consider how the major events in the history of redemption (salvation history) provide the framework for understanding any passage in the Old Testament.
- How do the major themes such as exodus, temple and Davidic kingship point to the fact that the Old Testament testifies to Christ?
- You may need to spend time working over the idea that Old Testament people and events foreshadow Christ.

Tip: As you read the narratives, ask yourself what we are being told about what God is doing.

7

Finding Christ in Genesis

The first five books of the Old Testament were traditionally attributed to Moses. Jesus accepted this tradition; Luke tells us that, after his resurrection, Jesus appeared to the two disciples on the road to Emmaus: 'beginning with Moses and all the Prophets, he interpreted to them in all the scriptures the things concerning himself' (Luke 24:27). John records a dispute Jesus had with some Jews. Jesus responds to them thus: 'There is one who accuses you: Moses, on whom you have set your hope. For if you believed Moses, you would believe me; for he wrote of me' (John 5:45–46). According to Jesus, then, the books of Moses (the Pentateuch) are about Jesus. Therefore, we are not only justified in attempting to discover how Genesis is about Jesus, we are required to do so.

> The structure and contents of Genesis lay the foundation for the entire biblical story and revelation of the kingdom of God.

The importance of the book of Genesis cannot be overestimated. The structure and contents of Genesis lay the foundation for the entire biblical story and revelation of the kingdom of God. Here we are introduced to:

- Creation.
- The fall of humanity into sin.
- The covenant of grace.
- Abraham as the father of the chosen people of Israel.
- The promise of a land for God's people.
- The beginnings of a theology of mission.
- The foreshadowing of kingship in humanity's control over creation.
- The prediction of the Egyptian captivity.

All of the major themes that I have dealt with in chapter 6 have their foundations in the book of Genesis. There is no need to repeat the outlines that I proposed there for those themes.

To understand Genesis, we need to explore its structure and storyline. As the narrative of Genesis proceeds, various characters and events are introduced that together make for a coherent plot.

Creation sets the stage for the action of the sovereignty of God, whose creative word points us ultimately to the redemptive Word who is the creator and who becomes flesh (John 1:1-3, 14). We see that humankind is defined first by a relationship with God and then with each other and the rest of creation. The temptation and rebellion of humanity bring judgement upon, and the confusion of, those relationships. The narratives contained in Genesis 4—11 highlight the need for God's grace to be revealed. The covenant with Abraham follows, and the path to redemption by grace is progressively revealed. As we consider some specific texts in Genesis, remember that our major goal is to find how the Old Testament points us to Christ. How it speaks of us is a derivative of that.

Genesis 14:17-24

After his return from the defeat of Chedorlaomer and the kings who were with him, the king of Sodom went out to meet him at the Valley of Shaveh (that is, the King's Valley). And Melchizedek king of Salem brought out bread and wine. (He was priest of God Most High.) And he blessed him and said,
'Blessed be Abram by God Most High,
Possessor of heaven and earth;
and blessed be God Most High,
who has delivered your enemies into your hand!'
And Abram gave him a tenth of everything. And the king of Sodom said to Abram, 'Give me the persons, but take the goods for yourself.' But Abram said to the king of Sodom, 'I have lifted

my hand to the Lord, God Most High, Possessor of heaven and earth, that I would not take a thread or a sandal strap or anything that is yours, lest you should say, "I have made Abram rich." I will take nothing but what the young men have eaten, and the share of the men who went with me. Let Aner, Eshcol, and Mamre take their share.'

Remember the three basic dimensions of the Bible that we must take account of:

- Literature.
- History.
- Theology.

Let us take these in turn, bearing in mind that the literary and the historical are subservient to the theological, that is, to God's revelation. Also bear in mind the interaction of these three dimensions. Remember that we are primarily concerned with understanding how this text points us to Christ, and testifies to his saving work.

1 Literature

While some would want to write off this passage, along with all that it is part of, as fictional myth or saga, it is clear that the writer intends it to be read as historical narrative. The details are clear and coherent.

2 History

Of course, under the rules of modern history writing, we cannot verify this as an event that actually happened. Whatever reservations a modern reader may have, we have to recognise that God's word sets it out as historical. Most importantly, we can look at this narrative for its theology within the context of the wider Abraham narrative.

3 Theology

This is not the place for an attempt at an exhaustive treatment of the passage. I will point out some of the salient points. A coalition of rulers of cities capture the city of Sodom and take Abram's nephew Lot captive. Abram takes a small army and rescues Lot. Two kings and two cities are introduced into this narrative: the king of Sodom and the king of Salem. The latter, Melchizedek, comes out to meet Abram as he returns from the battle. He is identified as a priest of God Most High. He blesses Abram who, in return, gives him a tenth of all his spoils of war. Melchizedek is king of Salem, generally understood as the ancient Jerusalem. He is a priest of Abram's God Most High.

In stark contrast to this honorific exchange between Abram and Melchizedek is the attempt of the king of Sodom, the evil city, to find favour with Abram. Abram refuses to take anything from him, and we later learn of the destruction of Sodom (Genesis 18—19). The significance of Salem is put on hold in the biblical story until we get to David. Jerusalem becomes the city of God where God's king rules and the temple stands. Rule and reconciliation emanate from God's city. The unusual nature of Melchizedek's authority is later applied to the Messiah (Psalm 110:4; Hebrews 7:21). Babylon is allowed to destroy Jerusalem because of its idolatry. Jesus comes as the new king and the new temple. Revelation describes the final destruction of the evil city of Babylon and the coming of the new Jerusalem from heaven.

This book is not intended to be a commentary on the whole of the Old Testament. Using the principles laid out so far, read and consider the following passages. Think about the meaning of the

> We should avoid the temptation to go first to an application to ourselves of the meaning of the text.

text, and then try to understand the theological significance of the events and people. Avoid the temptation to go straight to some kind of application to yourself. That comes later. Remember that we are dealing with the book of the acts of God.

Genesis 23:1–20

This is the account of Sarah's death and the problem Abraham had in finding a place to bury her. The points to ponder here are:

- This is the land promised to Abraham but he doesn't have possession.
- He must haggle with foreigners over the price of a plot within his own land.
- The promises of God about the land seem to be compromised.
- Abraham must learn afresh that he lives by faith in the promises of God.

The temptation is to apply this immediately to ourselves, for 'we walk by faith not by sight' (2 Corinthians 5:7). And, of course, it does point ultimately to that truth that we are yet to arrive in the place promised to us in Christ. The reason we should not simply focus on Abraham and his faith or his disappointments is that he has a theological significance that is not carried by him alone. He is the recipient of the covenant promises. In this passage, it is the promise of the land that is in focus. The theological theme, then, is not the man Abraham, but the promised land. Abraham figures as God's chosen one who is not yet in the promised land; he is in exile. Thus, we can track the path of this theme:

- Adam and Eve were in exile from Eden.
- Abraham is in exile from the land promised in the covenant.
- Israel enters the land, but maintaining possession is in doubt.
- It becomes clear that Canaan is not the ultimate land of promise.
- The exile into Babylon highlights the fact that God's people are still in exile.
- The return from Babylon really changes little.
- Jesus comes as the descendant of Abraham and David but to an alien sin-torn world.
- He comes to share our exile and to do what is necessary for us to be brought to the true land.

Genesis 50:22–26

The account of Joseph's death again points us in the direction of the covenant. It will lead to the exodus as the pattern of the redemption that will be needed to bring God's people into the true promised land, the kingdom of God. It also points us to the theme of the promised land. Note the reference to the promises to Abraham in verse 24.

Summary

Don't get stuck on the characters, good or bad. Look behind them for the plan and purpose of God involved in their doings and experiences. Get used to looking for the *main themes* even if the text in question is rather obliquely related to one or other of them. Then ask yourself how this theme relates to the progressive revelation that leads us to Christ.

Key note
The book of Genesis is the foundation for the entire theology of the Bible. It establishes the central focus on creation, sin and salvation. These themes are shown their true significance in Christ's saving work.

Take a moment to reflect…

- Read Psalm 8. How does it indicate the significance of the creation narrative?
- Ponder Genesis as a structured narrative about God and his purposes for the whole of creation, including the human race.
- What themes in Genesis would you nominate as most prominent in foreshadowing Christ?

Tip: Think of Genesis as a history of God's covenant with the people he created in his image.

8

Finding Christ in Israel's history

Christianity is a historical faith. God is not only Lord over all history but, in Jesus Christ, he entered into world history to bring salvation. Long before the Greeks Herodotus and Thucydides (fifth century BC), the pioneers of so-called 'scientific' history, Israel's historians had documented the events that are recorded in the Bible. Historians regard history writing as scientific when it is based solely on the evidence of documents, artefacts and other observable evidence.

> The events of Israel's history foreshadow the coming of the kingdom of God: the main character is God himself.

Thus, a history that puts God at the centre and claims revelation of a supernatural kind is not taken too seriously by secular historians. But, since God is the Lord of history and governs the events of his universe, we must allow him to reveal what he wills about those events even when they are beyond ordinary historical research. It is a reasonable assumption that the Israelites recorded their history starting with creation because of their God-given conviction that the story takes place in space and time. That is, they are not concerned with abstract ideas or even ideals, but with what God has done and what he has said about what he has done. Such history may include future events if God chooses to reveal them ahead of time.

Of first importance is the need to recognise that the historical books of the Bible are not written merely to record events. In fact, no history is. Every historian must be selective in the focus chosen for treatment. We have political histories, military histories, economic histories and so on. Historians then try to link cause and effect and even to suggest meaning for the events. The biblical books are theological histories: their main character is God. That is probably why the Jewish canon of the Old Testament classifies the books of Joshua, Judges, Samuel and Kings as the 'former prophets'. Remember that the events in Israel's history foreshadow the coming of the kingdom of God both in blessing and judgement.

Biblical history begins with creation and the subsequent events, leading to the person of Abraham, who is the father of the nation of Israel. The history of Israel as a nation begins with the descent of the sons of Jacob (Israel) into Egypt. The major events can then be enumerated as follows (Old Testament books in brackets):

1 Captivity and exodus (Exodus).
2 The giving of the law (Exodus, Leviticus, Numbers, Deuteronomy).
3 Entry into and possession of the promised land (Joshua).
4 The development of oversight in the land under the Judges, Samuel and Saul (Judges, 1 Samuel).
5 Kingship of David (2 Samuel, 1 Chronicles).
6 City of God (2 Samuel).
7 Temple (1 Kings).
8 Decline and exile to Babylon (1 and 2 Kings, 2 Chronicles).
9 Release from Babylon and post-exilic statehood (Ezra, Nehemiah).

Captivity and exodus

In retrospect, we can see that the significance of the captivity in Egypt and the exodus is that there can be no entry into the land of promise without a mighty redemption that God achieves for his people. Theologically, then, we can understand the Egyptian captivity as an expression of the human captivity to sin, Satan and death in that it negates every

> The exodus from Egypt provides the biblical foreshadowing of the redemption from captivity to sin through the saving work of Christ.

promise of God for his people to live under his rule in the land he will give them. The plagues in Egypt show the other side of the situation:

the one who would enslave God's people experiences judgements that mock his gods and threaten the very order of the creation that sustains his nation.

Israel's release is not merely a matter of being let go by the king of Egypt. The miracles of the plagues come to a climax in the tenth plague and in the fact that Israel cannot simply walk out of Egypt. The Passover sacrifice leads to a final miracle that occurs in the Red Sea as God's people cross on dry land and the armies of Pharaoh are destroyed.

The theological themes involved that point us to Christ are:

- Captivity that denies God's people life in the presence of God.
- Redemption through judgement and the release of God's people.

It is vital to note that the relationship of these events to the salvation we have in Christ is not merely illustrative or an analogy of ideas. In chapter 1, I pointed out the actual organic relationship between these events and the work of Christ. This is the gospel in prototype, such that those Israelites who responded to God's word and actions in faith were undoubtedly saved by the yet-to-come work of Christ. But further to that is the benefit to us to have this graphic real-life foreshadowing of what it is that Jesus has done for us.

The giving of the law

There are a number of things to remember when reading the law of Moses. First, and most important, is the fact that the law is given subsequent to the gracious saving acts of God in bringing Israel out of Egypt. Salvation came first as an act of God's grace.

> The Sinai law was a temporary measure to instruct the redeemed Israelites how to live as God's people.

The law was given to set out the appropriate response of God's people to his covenant of grace. They could not expect the favour of God if they choose to disobey and turn to idolatry. Over and over again the law is reinforced by reference to the fact that God brought them out of Egypt and set before them the prospect of entering the promised land (e.g. Exodus 19:4–5; 20:2; 22:21; 29:45–46; 33:1; Leviticus 11:45; 19:34; 22:31–33; 25:38; 26:3–13; Deuteronomy 5:15; 6:12–15, 20–25, etc.)

When you read the relevant passages dealing with the law (Exodus 20—40; Leviticus; most of Numbers; Deuteronomy), you may find it tedious and be tempted to give up. Don't try to figure out all the details. Remember this is the structure of life for Israel: a set of rules appropriate to their situation at that time. It is the fact of the law and its theological purpose, rather than the details, that should be our first focus. Take some comfort that the apostle Paul reminds us that the law is a temporary thing until Christ shall come (see Galatians 3:15–26). You may therefore wonder why, if it was a temporary thing, we should bother with it at all. That is a reasonable question seeing that the New Testament tells us that in Christ we are no longer under law but under grace (see Romans 6:14).

What the law of Moses should do for Christians is show us that the recipients of God's grace must live as his people. Liberation from slavery does not mean that life henceforth is a free-for-all. The covenant with Abraham and then with Israel was at the same time both unconditional and conditional. It was unconditional in that God did not discuss it with Abraham or Israel, but graciously put it in place. It was not deserved and sinful humans would by nature reject it, such is our enmity against God. But the covenant was also conditional in that it calls for the response of faith and obedience. The covenant contains both blessings and curses (see Deuteronomy 28). In New Testament terms, we say that God justifies (accepts) the ungodly by faith alone (Romans 4:1–5); but those justified by faith alone will then demonstrate the fruits of justification in a sanctified life (Romans 6; Ephesians 2:4–10; Colossians 3; 1 John 2:2—3:24).

There is a real sense in which the law is summed up in the ten commandments, and the ten commandments are summed up in the first commandment. All these are fulfilled in Christ, who lives as the perfectly obedient Israelite without sin. In his life, he is the sinless Son for us (Romans 5:10). Thus, we can assert that Jesus lived for us the life we should live but can't; he died to pay the penalty for the sinful life we have lived (but shouldn't have).

The promised land: entry and possession

We have already considered this theme in relation to Abraham and to the exodus. It is an important theme in the historical narratives, and the complex nature of the storyline in the relevant books should not be allowed to obscure the main thread. As Joshua leads the people into the land and takes possession, you will not miss the constant ambiguity in the way the people disobey and break the covenant. The faithfulness of God is astounding as he perseveres with this people. Possession of the land involves dispossession of the nations already there. It is made clear that the apparently brutal onslaught by Israel is God's judgement on the wickedness of these nations. All God's judgements are deserved. At the same time, it is also made clear that Israel's possession depends on faithfulness to God.

Judges and Kings

The political shape of Israel is a theocracy: God rules. But God uses mediators both of his sovereign rule and of his provision for reconciliation with his sinful people. We have seen how Moses was first among the mediators of God's word. Thus, we have emerging in Israel the essential offices of

> David was God's anointed king; the messianic ruler who foreshadowed the coming rule of Jesus, the Son of David.

prophet, priest and king. All three represent the way God deals with his people: he speaks to them and reveals himself; he provides the sacrificial ministry for the forgiveness of sins; and he rules over them. All three are necessary; all three are related to the way God is bringing in his kingdom. We will see later how Jesus comes as the ultimately true prophet, priest and king.

The ministry of the judges of Israel was part of the historical process whereby God led his people through a transition from the prophetic function of Moses and then the priestly role of Aaron, to the time when one man represents the people of God and, at the same time, is the mediator of God's rule over them. This was the king chosen and anointed by God. All of these God-given functionaries point to Christ. That is why we should not be too quick to stop off and use them as examples pointing to or instructing ourselves. In a derived way they can function as examples, but that is not their primary meaning.

For a while the prophet Samuel functions in a way that seems to combine all three offices, but in time the specifics of kingship emerge. Saul's kingship is abortive because the people requested a king for the wrong reasons. Then, David is revealed as God's chosen one and the promise is made to his descendants after him: David's son is named son of God (2 Samuel 7:12–14). The pedigree of kingship goes through David and Solomon, despite the latter's unfaithfulness. The fact that Jesus is identified as the Son of David in his role as saviour is significant. I urge you, then, not to go astray by making David's slaying of Goliath a lesson for believers in slaying their own 'Goliaths'. The story in 1 Samuel 17 points us towards the anointed Son of David, Christ, doing for us what we could not do for ourselves. It is not a lesson in what we can do with a little bit of faith!

Jerusalem and the temple

In the same way that the theme of the people of God progresses through Adam, Abraham, Israel and David, to Jesus, so there is a progressing in the themes of Jerusalem and the temple. Here, we are dealing with the theological theme of the dwelling of God with his people. It begins in Eden, and appears to come to an abrupt end with the expulsion from Eden. But God's grace intervenes and so the theme of God being with his chosen people, even in their exile, is a prominent one.

Cities are a fact of life; it is how human beings organise themselves for work and safety. But they are also centres of institutionalised evil and the rejection of God. Despite this propensity to concentrate evil, God gave the cities of the Canaanites to his people with some stern warnings against imitating the idolatry that was there in abundance. Eventually, David captured and secured the Jebusite fortress of Jerusalem, brought the ark of the covenant into it and established it as the focus of the promised land. Then, Solomon built the temple, a permanent replacement of the transportable tabernacle. Thus, the land where God is pleased to dwell with his people centres on Jerusalem and the temple.

All these tangible signs of God's kingdom, that is, of his dwelling with his people in the place he appoints, are destroyed by the Babylonians. We shall see in chapter 10 how the prophets deal with this deprivation. In anticipation, you should by now be used to the idea that the destruction of all these things in Israel's history points us to the hope given by the prophets which, in turn, points us to fulfilment in Christ.

Destruction and exile

The historical narrative in Samuel, Kings and Chronicles hurtles to a humiliating conclusion with the destruction of Jerusalem and the temple, and with the deportation of a significant portion of the people. It is clear that the exile of God's people is not over yet. It is also clear that the biblical historians regard the whole process of decline and fall with great seriousness since they give us so much detail (see 1 Kings 11—2 Kings 25; 2 Chronicles 10—36). We should try to put ourselves in the place of believing Israelites at this time. It must have been a terrible experience to live in that period of decline from the glories of the kingdoms of David and Solomon. Everything was coming undone and, again, the covenant promises seemed once again to be under threat.

In light of our survey thus far, the question that may well occur to us is how all this sin and covenant-breaking points us to Jesus. If Jesus fulfils the role of Israel, how do we explain the discrepancy between sinful Israel and sinless Jesus? I would suggest the following ways this corruption of the people of God should be viewed. After Genesis 3, we are all outside Eden. That goes for Abraham and his descendants. The exodus from Egypt may superficially seem to be leading to the total restoration of the kingdom of God among his people, but it is soon obvious that this is not the case. It is here that our discussion about typology is relevant. Israel in the promised land is a type of the people of God in his kingdom. Israel's idolatry and covenant-breaking, however, make it abundantly clear that their possession of Canaan is not an entry into the kingdom of God. There is an overall pattern involving redemption, entry, possession, city, temple and kingly rule. While this pattern points us to the kingdom of God, it is only a shadow and not the solid reality. What, then, can we say about the downside? How does that function as a type of the Saviour? It is an expression of utter corruption and sinfulness that is always under the condemnation of God and that will come under his judgement. That is the sinful Israel that Jesus, though without sin, became for Israel and for us. 'For our sake he made him to be sin who knew no sin, so that in him we might become the righteousness of God' (2 Corinthians 5:21). The only way Jesus could bear the sins of sinners was to be accounted as sinful in the Father's sight.

Summary

The history of the people of God from Adam through Abraham, and down to the Israelites in Canaan, provides a pattern of God's purposes for his kingdom and the way sinners can be included in it. It also provides the pattern of people under judgement for their rebellion against God. The failures of the people of God highlight the fact that the historical experience, as recorded in the Old Testament, is not an experience of the ultimate glories of God's kingdom. Old Testament history points us to a faithful Israelite, a true Son of God, who will take upon himself the judgement of sin and covenant-breaking.

Just as Israel's history was one of failure and rebellion against God, so our own personal histories betray the same sinful nature and rejection of God's rule over us. Jesus Christ came into this world to rewrite our histories by living the God-related life that we should live but can't. The whole of Old Testament history points to both the shape of a righteous life and the need for someone to provide it for us.

Key note
The historical framework of the Old Testament testifies to the saving work of Christ as providing for us a personal history that he himself lived on our behalf as a life that is acceptable to God.

Take a moment to reflect…

- Consider how the historical nature of the revelation of God shows us that Christianity is about God acting in history rather than being merely a set of ideals or moral teachings.
- Think about the gospel as Jesus providing for each believer a new history – his own – as the basis of our right standing with God.
- In thinking about the way the Bible applies to us, where do you consider that we fit into the history of salvation?

Tip: Remember that our acceptance with God is not grounded on how well we have lived, but upon the perfection of what Jesus has done for us.

9

Finding Christ in wisdom and psalms

The wisdom literature of the Old Testament is the term commonly used to refer to the books of Proverbs, Job and Ecclesiastes. It is probably appropriate to include also the Song of Songs. We need to try to understand why the terminology 'wisdom' has been applied to these documents and what it signifies.

Wisdom and the order of God's creation

There is an intriguing passage in Proverbs that may help us understand the biblical idea of wisdom. Here the abstract idea of wisdom is personified as the creator's aid in creation.

The Lord possessed me at the beginning of his work,
    the first of his acts of old.
Ages ago I was set up,
    at the first, before the beginning of the earth…
When he established the heavens, I was there;
    when he drew a circle on the face of the deep,
when he made firm the skies above,
    when he established the fountains of the deep,
when he assigned to the sea its limit,
    so that the waters might not transgress his command,
when he marked out the foundations of the earth,
    then I was beside him like a master workman,
and I was daily his delight,
    rejoicing before him always,

> rejoicing in his inhabited world
> > and delighting in the children of man.
>
> PROVERBS 8:22–23, 27–31

These passages speak of creation as planned by God in an orderly way so that there are limits and boundaries. In other words, it is not chaos and the order is perfect. This echoes the creation narratives in Genesis 1 and 2. In short, there is an orderliness in God's creation that reflects the person of God and his mind. Human wisdom, to be wisdom, must reflect the divine wisdom and function within it. Wisdom is about how we perceive and live by the order that God has established, even in our present world disordered by sin.

But the order of God's creation was not like that of a well-oiled machine. God did not create a mechanistic universe peopled by robots. Creation reflects God's personhood, and at its centre is the human element. God is the source of our personhood; we are made in his image. It is clear that God gave us humans brains and expects us to use them. This is clear from the fact that God holds us responsible for the way we respond to his wisdom. Wisdom is something we learn by experience which we then interpret by listening to God, who is the source of all wisdom.

> Wisdom is about how we perceive and live by the order that God has established, even in a world disordered by sin.

People will interpret their experience in a way that reflects the way they interpret the world. God-haters, and even those who are simply indifferent to God, will see themselves as autonomous, independent of God or gods. They themselves are the centre of their world and the reference point for their understanding of it. They will build a world view that ignores the reality of God and certainly rejects any idea of divine revelation. With these few introductory ideas in mind, let us try to make Christian sense of the Old Testament wisdom books.

There are a number of words that belong to the wisdom genre that indicate its concern with education and the use of the intellect. But education and intellectual activity are not treated for their own sake;

in fact, both can be used in a foolish and wicked way. Wisdom is often attributed to the simple, to the young and inexperienced. Note the words used in the preface to Proverbs:

> To know wisdom and instruction,
>   to understand words of insight,
> to receive instruction in wise dealing,
>   in righteousness, justice, and equity;
> to give prudence to the simple,
>   knowledge and discretion to the youth –
> Let the wise hear and increase in learning,
>   and the one who understands obtain guidance,
> to understand a proverb and a saying,
>   the words of the wise and riddles.
>
> PROVERBS 1:2–6

Notice the moral element in verse 3 as it speaks of righteousness, justice and equity. The more neutral vocabulary of this passage is likely to mislead us if we ignore the following verse (Proverbs 1:7):

> The fear of the Lord is the beginning of knowledge;
>   fools despise wisdom and instruction.

It is this that saves wisdom from being an amoral and purely secular shrewdness. The fear of the Lord is the reference point for all true wisdom. When it is lacking, wisdom becomes foolishness in God's sight.

The framework of wisdom

A world view is an idea of reality that each of us builds through reason and experience. Broadly speaking, there are two main ways people build their world views. The first is to see the universe as just happening, whether on account of a 'big bang' or of some other

> The fear of the Lord is the beginning of wisdom and true knowledge.

cause. The changes that occur in the universe and particularly in living things are regarded as due to massive periods of time plus chance and natural selection. The other position is to accept that the world as created by God in a way that reflects his very being. Here, the primary reference point is God himself and his word. This is as God intended it to be when he made human beings. In Genesis 1:26–28, God spoke to Adam and Eve and interpreted reality within which humans were to act responsibly. True wisdom, then, is the result of human experience interpreted in the light of God's revealing word. The overriding rule is: the fear of the Lord is the beginning of wisdom and true knowledge (Proverbs 1:7; 9:10). Because wisdom involves our relationship with God, the living source of wisdom, it takes on a moral dimension. It is more than worldly know-how and practical competence in life; it springs from a personal relationship with God.

The 'fear of the Lord' is a term that occurs often in the Old Testament. The word usually translated as 'fear' is not that used for terror, but it refers to a reverent awe for God's person and his will, such that we desire to be obedient. On the other hand, we must not so distance ourselves from what we usually term fear that we, in our own minds, domesticate God and regard him as our 'buddy'. God is Lord. He is king. He is judge of all. 'It is a fearful thing to fall into the hands of the living God' (Hebrews 10:29–31).

> Because true wisdom reflects God and his wisdom, there is always a moral dimension to being wise.

Wisdom must be understood in the light of who God reveals himself to be. The moral dimension is a personal dimension that reflects the holiness of God. That is why the book of Proverbs contrasts wisdom with foolishness, and righteousness with evil, in such a way as to make the two pairs synonymous. Thus, wisdom is to righteousness as foolishness is to evil (see Proverbs 10—15). This is important because it means that wisdom or folly (foolishness) are not functions of our IQ, and nor are righteousness and wickedness. They are moral dimensions that either reflect or repudiate the character of God. It also means that the way we use our reasoning powers and God-given intelligence is a spiritual matter.

The wisdom literature and the relevant historical narratives show us something of how the idea of wisdom developed during Israel's history.[8] We can also observe wisdom as it features in some of the prophetic passages about the future day of the Lord. But, before that, there is the downside as the prophets condemn the folly of apostate wisdom. Somewhere in Israel's history there appears to have been an institutionalising of wisdom with official wise men. Whether official or not, there is evidence that counsellors gave spurious advice, often with disastrous results. Solomon was the legendary wise man who fell from that grace. His son Rehoboam accepted foolish advice that led to the breakup of his kingdom (1 Kings 12). Isaiah condemns the wisdom of the wise men because of the hypocrisy of the people (Isaiah 29:13–16; 44:24–25). Jeremiah condemns the foolishness of the 'wise' (Jeremiah 8:8–9). God also condemns the false wisdom of pagans (Isaiah 19:11–12; Jeremiah 50:35–36; 51:57).

When Israel's wisdom is showing itself as folly and the nation is forsaking the Lord, then the prophets speak of one who will come to bring true wisdom to the people of God:

> The Lord is exalted, for he dwells on high;
>   he will fill Zion with justice and righteousness,
> and he will be the stability of your times,
>   abundance of salvation, wisdom, and knowledge;
>   the fear of the Lord is Zion's treasure.
> ISAIAH 33:5–6

Notice how that passage puts justice and righteousness in parallel with wisdom and knowledge, because they are due to the fear of the Lord. Isaiah also speaks of the messianic king from the house of David (the stump of Jesse, David's father) as the ultimate wise man:

> There shall come forth a shoot from the stump of Jesse,
>   and a branch from his roots shall bear fruit.
> And the Spirit of the Lord shall rest upon him,
>   the Spirit of wisdom and understanding,

> the Spirit of counsel and might,
> the Spirit of knowledge and the fear of the Lord.
> ISAIAH 11:1–2

If you read on in that oracle (Isaiah 11:1–9), you will see how this messianic wise man brings in the restored harmony of creation. God's order is restored.

If the fear of the Lord in the Old Testament involved a response of reverent trust to the word of God, then in the New Testament it must be faith in the Word of God incarnate, Jesus Christ. To put it another way: the gospel of Jesus is the reference point for true wisdom. This means that we interpret

> Proverbs assumes the universal perceptibility of the kind of orderly world that most of us experience for most of the time.

our experience and the world around us in the light of Jesus Christ. Meaning, for a Christian, is established by the fact that Christ is the wisdom of God who establishes all norms.

> … but to those who are called, both Jews and Greeks, Christ the power of God and the wisdom of God.
> 1 CORINTHIANS 1:24

> He [God] is the source of your life in Christ Jesus, whom God made our wisdom and our righteousness and sanctification and redemption.
> 1 CORINTHIANS 1:30, RSV

> I do not cease to give thanks for you, remembering you in my prayers, that the God of our Lord Jesus Christ, the Father of glory, may give you a spirit of wisdom and of revelation in the knowledge of him.
> EPHESIANS 1:16–17

> … that their hearts may be encouraged, being knit together in love, to reach all the riches of full assurance of understanding

and the knowledge of God's mystery, which is Christ, in whom
are hidden all the treasures of wisdom and knowledge.
COLOSSIANS 2:2–3

Paul refers to God's plan to unite all things in Christ (Ephesians 1:10).
And this Christ, the Word of God, created all things (John 1:1–3); thus
he is the author of truth and order. We must conclude, then, that
every fact of this universe, of all reality, is ultimately meaningful only
in the light of Christ. He made it. He redeems it. He will judge it. And,
finally, he will bring in the new heaven and the new earth.

Proverbs and the well-ordered life

Proverbs assumes the universal perceptibility of the kind of orderly
world that most of us experience for most of the time. Proverbs
contains three main types of wisdom sayings: the short, pithy,
proverbial sayings (e.g. Proverbs 10—15); longer instructions given
to a child or pupil (e.g. Proverbs 1:8—6:15); and numerical sayings
(e.g. Proverbs 6:16–19; 30:15–31). Each deals in their own distinct
way with the moral responsibility we have to learn to live by the
orderliness that God has established.

The key to much of Proverbs is the way different things, experiences
and activities actually have a common basis. It prompts us to search
for connections that we might not previously have appreciated.
Understanding how things connect and how they are disconnected
helps us to make wise decisions. While acknowledging the fact that
we live in a world skewed by sin, we can nevertheless work to discern
the way God has left the world liveable. Wisdom points to the fact
that our choices, our estimation of the world we live in and all our
relationships must be understood and overseen by the fear of the
Lord. It means that guidance is not an automatic prompting from
God, but comes from godly consideration of the circumstances
in the light of God's word. Because there is a connection between
deeds and outcomes, Proverbs emphasises natural retribution: act
foolishly, get a bad outcome; act wisely, get a good outcome.

Job and the reality of suffering

The book of Job asserts that order can sometimes remain hidden. It deals with the fact that life can now and again leave us with unanswerable questions and impenetrable mystery. While suffering and disaster are features of a fallen world due to human rejection of God, individual suffering is not always commensurate with the individual's actual sin. Job was a righteous man, but suffered incredible pain and loss. This is a book for the 'Why me?' syndrome. In many respects, it is about the quest of Job's 'friends' to discover why Job suffered so. They make a rigid application of the general rule that governs much of Proverbs: act foolishly and you will most likely suffer for it. But the common experience that the wisdom of Proverbs addresses is sometimes challenged by what is out of the ordinary.

> The book of Job asserts that order can sometimes remain hidden, leaving us with unanswerable questions and impenetrable mystery.

While Job could be said to be about suffering, at the centre of the book is the question 'Where is wisdom to be found?' (Job 28). Understanding human suffering and disaster requires wisdom. Job's companions have various answers to the problem of his suffering, but mainly the conclusion is that he must have deserved it because of some dreadful sin. Job's faith takes a battering, but he has occasional glimpses of hope (Job 19:25–27). Job's anguish is increased by what he perceives to be the silence of God. His ears are filled with the babbling of his misguided friends, yet God does not speak.

When God finally does speak, the desired answer to the problem of suffering is clearly not given. Our human yearning is to understand all mystery, but this is rejected as the darkening of counsel by words without knowledge (Job 38:2). A series of devastating rhetorical questions follow which remind us that the world was created and ordered by God's wisdom. Human wisdom is carved down to size (Job 38:4—40:2). Here is the lesson: God is the mighty sovereign Lord who works for the good of his people (Romans 8:18–25, 31–39). When Job repents (Job 42:1–6), it is not on account of the shameful sins of which his friends assume he must be guilty. It is for the sin of wanting to go beyond God's revelation and to penetrate the mysteries that God keeps to himself. It is for demanding to know 'Why?' when we suffer, rather than trusting the wisdom and goodness of God. Wisdom knows that there are bounds to our knowledge and understanding of God's sovereign purposes.

Ecclesiastes and apparent confusion

Ecclesiastes assumes that our perception of order can be confused by various spurious attempts to make sense of the world and of life. Ecclesiastes is not the easiest book to understand: on first sight, it is a bit of a 'dog's dinner'. Many see the author, Qohelet (or 'the preacher'), as showing how all human philosophies and world views fail. Sin has wrought so much confusion to human wisdom that it is futile. This has some strength as an explanation, but I would include among these failures a wooden and mistaken approach to Israelite wisdom, perhaps similar to the misguided wisdom of Job's friends. Qohelet's response to the apparent darkness, futility and vanity is to trust God and to receive our life as a gift.

Summary

Remember that the wisdom books are anchored to the covenant faith of Israel, even though this is not prominently referred to in the wisdom books themselves. It is an important messianic property (see 1 Kings 3—10). It is a feature of the rule of David, and is emphasised as being at the centre of Solomon's glorious rule. This fact alone

> Ecclesiastes warns against straying from God's wisdom and allowing the confusion caused by sin to rule our thinking.

puts the wisdom genre in the middle of the concerns of the covenant and Israel's salvation. Taken together, the wisdom books of the Old Testament present complementary perspectives on the subject of wisdom. Proverbs stresses the ability we have to perceive order even in a disordered world. Job points us to mysteries that can only be dealt with by a firm trust in the sovereign will of God and the understanding of his goodwill toward us. Ecclesiastes warns against straying from God's wisdom and allowing the confusion caused by sin to rule our thinking. Each in its own way prepares us for the fullest revelation of God's wisdom in Christ. Each gives a unique perspective on the need to recognise our own responsibility to think, to reason, to make decisions, but always in the framework or with the reference point of the gospel of Christ.

When Jesus comes to begin his ministry, we find him behaving like the wise men of old, but with a difference. We see this in the response to his conclusion to the sermon on the mount. Here, he uses the typical proverbial style of contrasting the wise man and the foolish man (Matthew 7:24–27). Note Matthew's subsequent comment:

> And when Jesus finished these sayings, the crowds were astonished at his teaching, for he was teaching them as one who had authority and not as their scribes.
> MATTHEW 7:28–29

The scribes were the successors of the wise men, but they lacked the authority that Jesus possessed as the source of wisdom. Jesus also used the wisdom forms of parables and proverbs in teaching his wisdom. Judaism and Rabbinic theology began to go wrong when they rejected Jesus as the promised Messiah and thus as the reference point for wisdom.

The psalms: songs about Jesus

Many of the psalms were written by David from his own perspective. Jesus is the Son of David and fulfils the role of David as the anointed king of God's people. Other psalms were written by godly Israelites and apply to Israel. Jesus is the true Israel, the representative and perfect man of God. These considerations alone should caution us against a simple one-to-one identification of ourselves with the psalmists and their songs. All the psalms are fulfilled, in various ways, in Jesus. Our connection with the psalms, then, is made by being in union with Christ by faith. Does this matter? I think it matters a lot. If we fail to see that our connection with anything in the Old Testament is only through our being 'in Christ', then we are in effect assuming that we can have fellowship with God the Father even when bypassing Jesus.

The New Testament contains more quotes from, and references and allusions to, Psalms and Isaiah than to any other Old Testament book. A number of the quotes are directly applied to Jesus as the Messiah. For example, Psalm 2:1–2 is interpreted as about the Christ in Acts 4:25–26; and Psalm 2:7 is applied to Christ in Acts 13:33, Hebrews 1:5 and 5:5. Psalm 8:4–6 is applied to Jesus in Hebrews 2:5–9. Peter (in Acts 2:25–28) quotes Psalm 16:8–11 as referring to Christ's recurrection. Psalm 110 is quoted some 18 times in the New Testament. One estimate is that there are 14 messianic psalms referred to in the New Testament.

> When considering application, the first question we should ask about any part of the Old Testament is, 'How does this text testify to Jesus?'

One point that I must repeat is that Jesus does not fulfil only uniquely obvious messianic scriptures. He fulfils all scripture. If the psalm you are considering contains the words of, or is addressed to, the Messiah, or if the speaker is an unnamed Israelite, the focus is the same. This is because the Messiah was the one for the many: he represents the whole of God's people. Jesus came as the true representative of the people of God. Thus, when considering application, the first question we should ask about any part of the Old Testament is: 'How does this text testify to Jesus?' Then, since a Christian is 'in Christ', we can ask about its application to us. Let us now look at a couple of psalms and see how the links are made with the New Testament.

Psalm 22: a lament that turns to praise

This psalm has an obvious link with Jesus since he utters part of it on the cross (Mark 15:34). The psalm is a lament of an individual, identified as David, and its context can only be guessed at. It is remarkable for the many ways it anticipates the details of Christ's sufferings (e.g. vv. 7–8, 16–18). When we get to verse 22 there is an abrupt change from lament to confidence and praise. Something has happened to cause this reversal of fortune. In David's case, it is not death and resurrection, but the psalm does point to the Son of David who did suffer like this, even to death, but was raised from the dead and exalted on high.

A lament is something we find quite often in the Old Testament. There are other songs of lamentation, and there is a whole book called Lamentations. There are many songs of praise also and, in the case of Psalm 22, lament and praise are connected intimately. The point we must remember is that any song of a godly Israelite, or of a group of them, points us to the one true Israelite, the Son of David.

Psalm 23: the shepherd psalm

Possibly the best-known psalm of all provides food for thought and a challenge to understand its testimony to Jesus. Because there is a 'soft' side to the idea of a shepherd, this psalm is easily adapted in the secular mind to a rather poorly defined idea of the messianic theme. In Isaiah 40:11, the Lord is spoken of as the shepherd who 'will gather the lambs in his arms', and who will 'gently lead those that are with young'. But there is another dimension to the shepherd imagery. The rulers of Israel were false shepherds who did not tend the flock (e.g. Jeremiah 23:1–2; 25:34–38; Ezekiel 34:1–10). They brought destruction to themselves and their people. The mercy of God is in promising to set good shepherds over his faithful people (Jeremiah 23:5–6; Ezekiel 34:11–23). The good shepherd is the good ruler over his flock. The imagery is powerful and not sentimental. When Jesus declares that he is the good shepherd, he combines the two aspects: sovereign rule and saving love (John 10:11–18).

Psalm 23 anticipates the king of Israel coming as saviour and ruler. David was himself a shepherd, so the terminology comes from his own experience. Indeed, it may be this that led to the use of shepherd imagery for the rulers of Israel. Ideally, the king was to rule by God's word, and not to lift up his heart above his brethren (Deuteronomy 17:18–20). But he was to be a ruler. Shepherds ruled their flock using the rod and staff (Psalm 23:4). Only by power could he deal with the enemies of his flock (v. 5). The mercy spoken of in verse 6 is the covenant love of God for his people (see comments below on Psalm 136). To dwell in the house of the Lord forever is not a vague reference to some happy afterlife that can be moulded to fit any self-made notion of heaven. The house of the Lord could only be entered by those who were cleansed of sin by atoning sacrifice. The psalm thus points to the new temple who is our Immanuel (John 2:19–21; Ephesians 2:19–22).

Psalm 46: a Zion psalm

Zion is the name frequently given to Jerusalem, especially in the Psalms and prophets when speaking of the place of the city in the saving work of God. Other Zion psalms are Psalms 48, 76, 87 and 122 (see also Isaiah 40:9; 41:27; 46:13; 51:3, 11). Psalm 46 is the basis for Luther's famous hymn, 'A Mighty Fortress is Our God'. I return to the points made earlier about God dwelling with his people. In this regard, the city and the temple really become alternate ways of expressing this presence of God (see v. 5). So, the confidence is that 'the Lord of hosts is with us' (vv. 7, 11). Jesus is the new temple (John 2:19–21) and thus also fulfils the role of Zion. He is Immanuel: God with us.

Psalm 51: a psalm of repentance

This psalm is under a heading that places it in the context of David's repentance over his adultery with Bathsheba. It is a sustained expression of regret and an admission of

> Jesus fulfils the whole of the Old Testament, not just the good bits.

guilt. David asks for mercy and cleansing. The obvious question concerns the application of this psalm to Jesus, the sinless Son of God. Let me remind you again that Jesus fulfils the whole of the Old Testament, not just the good bits. When he was baptised with John's baptism of repentance, he identified with a sinful people. Of what did he repent if he had no sin? This was probably in John the Baptist's mind when he objected to Jesus lining up for baptism (Matthew 3:13–15). Jesus stood for Israel. Remember that repentance has two sides: turning from sin and turning to God. Jesus was the most 'God-turned' Israelite that ever lived. His repentance justifies our imperfect repentance. To do this he had to 'be made sin for us'.

Psalm 136: a salvation-history psalm

There are several psalms that focus on the saving deeds of God: for example, Psalms 78, 106, 107, 114 and 136. One way that Israel praised God was simply to tell the story of what he had done to save his people. This psalm is unique in that every verse repeats the same refrain: 'For his steadfast love endures forever.' The narrative of the psalm, which occurs in the first half of every verse, begins and ends with a call to thanksgiving (vv. 1–4, 26) and then proceeds to acknowledge God as creator (vv. 5–9), redeemer (vv. 10–16) and giver of victory (vv. 17–25). The constant refrain points to the fact that every detail of Israel's life, from creation to conquest, is due to God's covenant faithfulness. The word translated 'steadfast love' in the ESV (KJV 'mercy'; NIV 'love') is a rather technical word in the Old Testament that has strong connections with the covenant (Hebrew, ḥesed). It means the faithfulness of God to keep his covenant with his people. Everything the people of God experience, from A to Z, is due to God's covenant love and faithfulness, and should evoke profound and continual thanksgiving. The Christian equivalent is to recount the deeds of Christ in the gospel and give thanks. It is more than an analogy: the old covenant finds its fulfilment in the new covenant that Jesus establishes.

Key note

The wisdom literature and the Psalms express the human response to the world and daily life in the light of who God is and what he has revealed of himself by word and deed. Thus, 'the fear of the Lord is the beginning of wisdom and knowledge'. These books point to Christ as our wisdom and our response to God.

Take a moment to reflect…

- Wisdom, especially Proverbs, teaches us that we are responsible for our actions.
- How does 'the fear of the Lord' show that God has given us the freedom to act within the framework of his revelation?
- When we make a poor choice that backfires, how does it help to know that Christ is our wisdom?

Tip: The Psalms are written by David (a messianic figure) and other godly Israelites; there is thus good reason to think of them as the Psalms of Jesus. Our union with Christ by faith then enables us to think of them as ours.

10

Finding Christ in the prophetic books

There are many reasons why some Bible readers find the books of the prophets confusing. There are also reasons why some have a tendency to miss the real importance of the prophets and to misuse the texts. To avoid such confusion and misapplication, we need to understand who the prophets were and how they functioned in Israel.

Who were the prophets?

The prophets were men and women chosen by God to speak his word to his people and, for some of them, to share in the process of recording God's word in written form. Abraham is the first person referred to as a prophet (Genesis 20:7). God also appointed Aaron to be prophet for Moses in the coming conflict with Pharaoh (Exodus 7:1). Aaron was to be the spokesperson for the words God gave to Moses, but, as we have already seen, Moses is really the definitive

> The prophets were men and women chosen by God to mediate his word to his people.

prophet who establishes the pattern of the one appointed to be the mouthpiece of God to his people. He also is credited with having written down the bulk of the Pentateuch, the books of the law. Beyond that, we have no sure evidence that, up to the time of the writing prophets, the other prophets wrote anything. The non-writing prophets would include Deborah, Samuel, Nathan, Gad, Elijah and Elisha. Some scholars suggest Samuel was perhaps responsible for at least some of the material in the later historical narrative. There is no direct evidence for this.

There came a time in Israel's history when a new brand of prophet arose to whom it was given to produce written records of their preached oracles. They may not have written these books themselves, but someone did. For example, Jeremiah used a scribe, Baruch, to write his scroll, and to rewrite it after the king destroyed it (Jeremiah 36:4, 32). The result of this new prophetic activity is that we inherited the books we classify as latter prophets: Isaiah, Jeremiah, Ezekiel and the twelve minor prophets. Daniel is also a prophetic book, and is usually included with the latter prophets.

I believe it is safe to conjecture a reason for this new activity. Up to the time of Solomon, the pattern of salvation and of the kingdom of God had been revealed through the historical experience of God's people as it was interpreted prophetically.

> When the glory of Israel's historic kingdom faded, God had something new to say through the writing prophets.

All that needed to be written down for that period had been written in the Pentateuch, the five Books of Moses. After that, the prophetic function was to hold the people to what had already been revealed. But, after Solomon, the situation became dire as the nation split and both parts slid further into apostasy. The end of all the hopes based on the promises of God seemed to be imminent.

God's answer to this situation was given by the so-called writing prophets in the books referred to above. God had something new to say and these prophets were his mouthpiece. The difficulty in these books is mainly literary: the oracles of the writing prophets are almost all in poetry. Now, scholars disagree over what Hebrew poetry involves; it certainly isn't a matter of rhyme. One thing is clear: it involves the use of a great deal of repetition, parallelism,[9] poetic imagery, simile and metaphor. You may struggle to make sense of a lot of it, especially if you are more attuned to simple and straightforward prose. Let me try to simplify it a little for you.

All the writing prophets, either directly, or indirectly, contain three elements:[10]

1 They accuse their contemporaries concerning the immediate problem of apostasy, idolatry and overall covenant-breaking. This often involves pinpointing specific sins.

> The prophets spoke three main types of oracles: accusation of sin, threat of God's judgement and assurance of salvation.

2 They relay God's words of displeasure at their unfaithfulness and his threatened judgement.

3 They remind the people that God is both sovereign and faithful to his covenant promises. This means that, though judgement will consume the covenant-breakers, God will nevertheless bring about his purposes of establishing a faithful people in his kingdom.

These three kinds of oracles, then, need to be recognised: indictment of sin, threat of judgement and assurance of salvation for the faithful. Apart from some occasional historical or personal details, there is little else in the prophetic books. However, when you read the prophets you will notice that many of the oracles of judgement and of future restoration can be quite ambiguous as to whether the fulfilment is perceived as near and local, or far off and even universal in effect. This is due to the fact that, even when there is a partial fulfilment near at hand, the real fulfilment does not come until the New Testament. An example is the return from exile, which occurred after the decree of 538BC, but found its real fulfilment in Christ.

The next thing to notice is that the oracles of salvation, along with those of judgement, are based on historical experience of the past. These prophets recapitulate the pattern of salvation and the kingdom that has already been revealed in God's dealings

> The prophetic oracles of future salvation recall the past experiences of God's saving acts.

with his people, from the beginning of history up to the reign of Solomon. We dealt with this in chapter 5, and now might be a good time to revisit that discussion and refresh your mind on it. The point that was emphasised was that the prophetic view of what God will do in the future establishment of his kingdom will not be merely a replay of what has already happened and has failed. The prophets use the past pattern of events to project a future kingdom that will be perfect, glorious and eternal. This is important, because it means that the prophetic oracles do not imply that all the promises of the past have failed, and a new and completely different plan is now put in place. By recapitulating the past, they emphasise the permanence of God's original promises. The repeat of the pattern confirms the typology that is projected in the period of Old Testament history up to the time of Solomon.

The chronology of the latter prophets

It is important to remember that the writing prophets functioned when Israel's historical experience was in decline up to and during the period of the exile to Babylon. In the period after the return from exile, there are three prophets, Haggai, Zechariah and Malachi, who interpret the failure of the kingdom of God to arrive once the exiles returned home.

Often the prophets themselves identify the kings during whose reigns they prophesied. The apparent lack of systematic approach to the future hopes for the kingdom can be largely put down to the fact that the prophets addressed particular situations in the politics and covenant faithfulness (or unfaithfulness) of the people. Sometimes ancient chronology can be difficult to establish, but we can get a basic framework with more certainty in the later dates based on documentary evidence.

A suggested overall chronological outline, which involves some early estimates, would look like this (all dates are approximate and BC):

Abraham	1800
The exodus	1445
David	1000–961
Israel splits from Judah	922
Elijah and Elisha	mid ninth century

The writing prophets (southern kingdom unless otherwise indicated):

Joel	early eighth century
Hosea	760–722 (northern kingdom)
Amos	760 (northern kingdom)
Micah	742–700
Isaiah	740–700

Northern kingdom destroyed by Assyria 722

Nahum	664–620
Zephaniah	640–?
Jeremiah	627–580
Habakkuk	605

Babylonians besiege Jerusalem 597; destroy the city and temple 586

Ezekiel	593–570
Obadiah	587–585

Persian edict of return 538 (return of Jews and rebuilding begins)

Haggai	520
Zechariah	520
Malachi	460

Some of the prophets address the wider historical situation directly; some do this indirectly as they turn their attention to the internal spiritual problems of the people. When they do give words of assurance, they are usually about the restoration of the structures that existed in the height of Israel's glory and the events leading up to them.

An error to avoid in applying the message of the prophets

Among those whose approach to the Bible leans towards liberalism, or other derivatives of the 'Enlightenment' of the 18th century, a certain approach to the prophets often emerges. The supernatural element is generally downplayed or even simply dismissed. Predictive prophecy as divine revelation is disallowed as impossible. Prophecy is not regarded as controlled by the inspiration of the Holy Spirit; it is regarded as merely human comment on events as they occurred. The result is that if the prophetic indictments of the social evils in apostate Israel are to have any application to the present, they are transferred to speak to the ills of modern society. The distinctive role of Israel as God's chosen people is not acknowledged; it is merely one nation among many. For Israel, now read Britain, America or any other modern nation. From this perspective, making one's principal purpose in ministry to critique our contemporary society is often said to be 'prophetic'. It isn't.

As soon as I say that, some will (wrongly) read me as saying that modern social ills are irrelevant to the biblical message. That is not so. What we need to understand is that a 'social gospel' that regards evangelism as unnecessary, the inspiration of scripture as an illusion and sees the Christian mission as fulfilled solely in feeding the poor, housing the homeless and addressing the social ills of our time is a distortion of the biblical message. There is an important distinction to be made between such a social gospel that ignores sin, salvation and judgement, and the important social implications of the gospel as proclaimed in the New Testament.

I say again, London or New York or Jakarta are not Jerusalem. They do have in common that they are cities with all the problems of urbanisation. But the message of the prophets is not to strive 'until we have built Jerusalem in England's green and pleasant land'. I must emphasise that the message of the prophets does not point to a 'social gospel' that sees the essence of Christianity in social action. It points rather to the gospel of the doing and dying of Jesus Christ to reconcile us to God; a reconciliation that has great social implications but is certainly not exhausted by them.

The theology of the prophetic view of God's future acts

The letter to the Hebrews begins:

> Long ago, at many times and in many ways, God spoke to our fathers by the prophets, but in these last days he has spoken to us by his Son, whom he appointed the heir of all things, through whom also he created the world.
> HEBREWS 1:1–2

The Old Testament prophets spoke the divine word; and Jesus is the divine Word. The three dimensions of prophetic proclamation are linked to the specific historical situation that existed for both Israel and Judah. We have already looked at the way the major characters, events and institutions foreshadow the reality that will emerge with Jesus. Let me stress again: it is this foreshadowing that constitutes the link to Jesus Christ. We know God the Son is always present and he is later identified as the Word of God (John 1:1–2, 14). This implies that the Word that created the world, and came to Israel through the prophets, was the presence of God the Son. This is unavoidable. This is why Jude can identify Jesus as bringing Israel out of Egypt (Jude 5). But we are trying in this study to establish the way to identify how the Old Testament foreshadowed Jesus Christ in such a way that the faithful who grasped the shadow thereby grasped the reality. For Israel, grasping the shadow was a matter of believing the promises of God. We need to distinguish between the eternally present God the Son and his presence among us as the incarnate Son, Jesus Christ. The

> Jesus Christ was not only the definitive prophet who mediated God's word, he was that Word.

prophets foreshadow the latter. One way forward in this is to structure our understanding on the three dimensions of the prophetic message. Beginning with indictment, we must recognise both the similarities and the distinctions between then and now.

Prophetic accusations of sin (indictments) and Christ

Bear in mind that the standard that informs the prophets is the law of Moses and the saving acts of God. The context of the law is the specific saving work of God (covenant and exodus), and the establishment of his people in the promised land. There are some areas of overlap of the law with the notion of lawfulness in the New Testament, and there are some real distinctions. The main point of contact is the fact that God reveals to humanity his standards. The word of God established the standards from the moment God created Adam and Eve. The sin of humanity was then, and goes on being, a rejection of God's right to order his universe; to say what is right or wrong; to designate truth and error.

There is a clear overlap of Christian ethics with the ethical meaning of the law of Moses. That is not the issue. Right and wrong, truth and error, are definitively demarcated by Jesus Christ. Many of the infringements for which Israel was condemned no longer apply to us. On the other hand, there are many which still do apply, especially the breaking of ethical norms. When Paul reflects on this, he says that we are all condemned as sinners. The whole human race has rejected the truth that is in God and for this we are rightly condemned. The good news of the gospel includes this bad news: we are by nature children of wrath. But Jesus became sin for us (2 Corinthians 5:21).

The value of the prophetic accusations is not so much in every specific detail of law-breaking, but in the fact that, even when we are recipients of God's grace, we still go on expressing our sinful natures. The law

> The Old Testament law revealed to Israel the seriousness of sin and showed why Jesus needed to become sin for us.

demonstrates the seriousness of sin. The amazing faithfulness of God is seen as he continues to lead his people towards his kingdom even when they are disobedient. The bewildering lesson from the prophetic condemnations is that people continue to express their rebellion even when they have experienced the gracious mercy of God. Thus, we see Israel's idolatry that followed the saving event of the exodus from Egypt. Read the book of Judges and observe the cycle of waywardness of a people who have just experienced the saving deeds of one of the judges.

Oracles of judgement and Christ

It is easy to find prophetic words of judgement. They are everywhere and, for many, this can be a stumbling block. Very early in the history of the Christian church, comparisons were being made between the stern, condemnatory God of the Old Testament and the New Testament's God of love. People still make this unwarranted comparison today. Yet, there is so much in the Old Testament about the love of God that simply cannot be ignored. The love of God cannot be divorced from his judgement. If the kingdom of God is to be somewhere you want to be forever, the question of evil and evil people has to be dealt with. Right the way through the Bible, judgement is the other side of the coin to God's grace and love. We need to be clear that judgement is always deserved, but God's grace is free.

The other side to the distortion mentioned above is the idea that in the New Testament it is all sweetness and light. Yet, Jesus has as much to say about judgement as does the New Testament as a whole. For all those who believe in some kind of heavenly afterlife, there are two options to consider. Either God is judge who will cleanse his kingdom of all unrighteousness; or we will share 'heaven' with unrepentant terrorists, rapists, murderers and all the evil men and women of history. The gospel is about cleansing us of all unrighteousness through faith in Jesus Christ. The prophetic message of judgement on all who do not repent of their God-hating unbelief and evildoing is carried through strongly into the New Testament. For example, Matthew 3:7, 10, 12; 5:22, 29–30; 7:1, 13, 19; 10:28; 12:36–37; 25:31–46; Mark 16:16; Luke 3:9, 17; 13:3–5; John 3:16–18; 12:47–48; 16:8; Acts 13:40–41; Romans 2:1–8, 16; 5:9, 16–18; 2 Corinthians 2:15–16; 4:3–4; Ephesians 5:6; Colossians 3:6; Hebrews 9:27; 2 Peter 2:3–9, 3:7; Revelation 6:16–17; 19:15; 20:11–15, and many more.

The prophets, then, remind us of the seriousness of rebellion against the living God. Sometimes the specific aspects of Israel's sin and the consequent judgement are transferrable to the New Testament scene. The message above all is that God is judge of all the earth and we shall all be accountable for our lives. While most of the oracles of the prophets are directed at Israel and Judah, there are significant words directed at the nations of the world (e.g. Isaiah 13:1–22; 14:24–32; 15:1—19:15; 21:1–16; 23:1–18; 34:1–17; Jeremiah 46—51; Ezekiel 25—32). Thus, Paul can say that 'all, both Jews and Greeks [Gentiles], are under sin, as it is written: "None is righteous, no, not one"' (Romans 3:9–10).

Above all, the prophetic view of God's judgement points us to the judgement of the cross of Christ. Jesus bore our justly deserved judgement so that we might go free. It is a gift of God and involves the great exchange:

> For our sake he [God] made him [Christ] to be sin who knew no sin, so that in him we might become the righteousness of God.
> 2 CORINTHIANS 5:21

> For while we were still weak, at the right time Christ died for the ungodly. For one will scarcely die for a righteous person – though perhaps for a good person one would dare even to die – but God shows his love for us in that while we were still sinners, Christ died for us.
> ROMANS 5:6–8

Prophetic oracles of salvation and Christ

It is time now to revisit the analysis of the prophetic message and how it recapitulates the historical experience of God's people: see Table 1 (pp. 50–51) and Table 2 (pp. 52–53) in Chapter 5. We can now examine the way Jesus is the fulfiller of these categories that dominate and shape the redemptive history, and the prophetic projection of these into a future day of the Lord. Again, I must emphasise that there are some who would reject completely my understanding of Christ the fulfiller and write it off as 'replacement theology'.[11] This is one of the most disputed areas of biblical interpretation. I can only respectfully reply that I do not see it as 'replacement theology' but 'fulfilment theology'. I believe this is the only way to be true to the New Testament.

> We must allow Jesus in his gospel to show us how the prophetic oracles of the Old Testament are fulfilled.

There are two main ways the matter is approached. First, there are those who construct a historical timeline on the basis that prophetic oracles must be interpreted absolutely literally. They then have to fit the expected future events involving the return of Jesus into this timeline. The result is often an almost moment by moment prediction of what is going to happen, and even when it will happen. Second, there is the position I have worked with since my first contacts with biblical theology. This is to start with Jesus as God's final and fullest revelation. Jesus claims to be the new temple, so it makes no sense to propose that the prophets force us to expect another temple in Jerusalem. The apostles apparently had no difficulty in asserting a 'fulfilment theology' as Peter does in Acts 2:16–35, and Paul in Acts 13:32–35. Paul finds all the promises of God have their 'Yes' in him (2 Corinthians 1:20). According to Hebrews 12:22–24, Zion is not some place on this earth that Christians will come to in the future, for they are already there in Christ.

I say again: we must allow Jesus in his gospel to show us how the prophetic oracles of salvation are fulfilled. Literalism ignores symbol and imagery. It asserts that, sometime in the future, the temple will be rebuilt in Jerusalem even though there is no hint of this in the New Testament. By requiring a literal temple in a literal Jerusalem and a literal return of Jews to Palestine, this approach has robbed Jesus of his role of fulfiller of these promises. This is important because it makes the gospel-work of Jesus both imperfect and incomplete.

Some prophetic passages to consider

Isaiah 1:21—2:5

This passage may involve two distinct oracles (Isaiah 1:21–31 and Isaiah 2:1–5) but, taken together, they express the three kinds of oracle described above. First, the indictment of sin in 1:21–23; then the threat of judgement in 1:24–25, 28–31; and, finally, the promise of salvation in 1:26–27 and 2:1–5. Notice, also, the terminology of the oracles of salvation: they focus on Zion (i.e. Jerusalem as the city of God). Zion is the earthly focal point of God's kingdom and the place where he expresses his dwelling with his people. The obvious question is, where is this Zion that will be the fulfilment of these prophecies? One important answer is given in Hebrews 12:18–24: Zion is where Jesus is. Zion and temple go together. Jesus is the new temple and, by faith, we are united to him and are built into the new temple (Ephesians 2:18–22).

Jeremiah 23:1–8

The condemnation is here levelled at the shepherds, that is, the rulers, of Israel. They have caused the flock to be scattered. The threat, though brief, is ominous (v. 2b). The assurance of salvation is full of grace. God will gather his people and set good shepherds over them (vv. 3–4). This good rule will be exercised by a branch for David whose name, significantly, is 'The Lord is our righteousness' (vv. 5–6). This amazing oracle points us to the Good Shepherd who becomes for us our righteousness (John 10:11–16, 27–30; Romans 3:21–23; 1 Corinthians 1:30; 2 Corinthians 5:21).

Ezekiel 36:22–38

This passage is remarkable, firstly, for the emphasis on the fact that the salvation of God's people vindicates the holiness of his name (vv. 22–23, 32). Secondly, salvation involves both the bringing of the saved to God's place (vv. 24, 28–31, 33–35), and the cleansing from sin (vv. 25, 29). The cleansing is spoken of in terms of a ceremonial sprinkling and a Spirit-regenerated heart (vv. 25–27). The images of regeneration, water and Spirit are the likely source of Jesus' words to Nicodemus in John 3:5–8. Again, we see the commonly used prophetic theme of a return to the promised land. God will take them and bring them into the kingdom. This, and many passages like it, points us to the gospel. Paul can say that when we are in Christ by faith, he has already brought us home (Ephesians 2:4–6; Colossians 3:1–4). And remember how Hebrews 12:22–24 reminds Jewish Christians that, in Christ, they are already there.

Joel

The prophecy of Joel is difficult to date since it concentrates on the future events revealed by God and gives little by way of its own historical context. The big theme is the future 'day of the Lord'. This is the name given to the time when God will demonstrate his righteousness in final acts of judgement and salvation. The day of the Lord is to be feared by an unrepentant and unfaithful people. Catastrophe has already befallen them (Joel 1:1–12). God calls them to repent (Joel 1:13–14), for the day of the Lord is near (Joel 1:15—2:11). If they return to the Lord, they will find mercy and experience the steadfast love of God (his covenant faithfulness). This covenant faithfulness is revealed in the way God has already shown pity in so many ways (Joel 2:18–27). The day is coming when the Lord will pour out his Spirit on his people, but will judge the peoples of the earth who have opposed the coming of his kingdom

(Joel 2:28—3:21). If you look at Acts 2:16–21, you will see how the apostle Peter interprets this promise of God's Spirit as fulfilled on the day of Pentecost. Notice also that he goes on to apply Psalm 16 to the resurrection of Jesus, and in Acts 2:29–31 he refers to 2 Samuel 7:12–14 as also fulfilled by the resurrection of Jesus.

What shall we do with Jonah?

'Heave him overboard!' you might say. But, as the book reminds us, that is not the answer since God has ways and means of getting his servants to the right place at the right time. Jonah's encounter with a great fish ensures that he eventually gets to Nineveh, the capital of the Assyrian empire. His preaching evokes a positive reaction of repentance that averts God's judgement. Jonah is not pleased that this pagan city is spared and the book ends with God's rebuke of the prophet. Strange. What is more, 2 Kings 14:25 puts Jonah in the eighth century – not long before the Assyrians destroyed Samaria and ended the northern kingdom of Israel. So what is the message? The only reference to the book in the New Testament is the statement of Jesus in Matthew 12:38–41 in which he castigates the scribes who asked him for a sign. He replies that the only sign will be the sign of Jonah, that is, the resurrection of the Son of Man.

So, if the men of Nineveh repented as Jesus said (v. 41), what kind of repentance was it that allowed them so soon to invade Israel and destroy it? Jesus asserts that the men of Nineveh will rise up in judgement on the Jews who are rejecting Jesus and the kingdom of God. This suggests that these events and the message of Jonah are directed at apostate Israel to remind them that 'not all Israel are Israel' (Romans 9:6–8); and that 'God is able from these stones to raise up children for Abraham' (Matthew 3:9). Of course, we can read this book for personal lessons about obedience and the sovereignty of God, but the message, I believe, is wider than that.

Malachi

Malachi is the last book in our Old Testament but not in the Hebrew Bible, which puts the section called 'Writings' last. Nevertheless, Malachi is a fitting ending to the Old Testament as one of the three post-exilic prophets. He anticipates the events that we read of in the Gospels, especially the ministry of John the Baptist. The post-exilic community exhibited much the same kinds of problems that had brought about the exile in the first place. Malachi focuses on a corrupt priesthood and the profaning of the covenant in general. What the Jews seek in the restoration of God's temple will, in fact, be a day of judgement and cleansing. For the evildoers, it will be a day of destruction, but for those who fear the Lord's name, 'the sun of righteousness will rise with healing in its wings' (Malachi 4:2).

Key note
The prophets speak God's word, indicting sin, predicting judgements and proclaiming God's faithfulness to the covenant as they speak of future restoration, blessing and the coming of God's kingdom. In this, they foreshadow the day of Christ.

Take a moment to reflect…

- Can you give a good reason for the prophets to portray the future in terms of the past?
- Can you express your understanding of how the New Testament sees the fulfilment of prophecy in Christ?
- How do the covenant promises and threats announced by Moses structure the writings of the prophets?

Tip: Allow Jesus and the New Testament writers to show us how prophecy is fulfilled.

11

Jesus Christ the fulfiller

Because Christ is God's final and fullest word of revelation, we began this survey with Christ so that we might end with Christ. Thus, I have really been writing this chapter from the start of the book. We should be in a position now to understand better why and how the New Testament writers drew together all the lines that connect Jesus to the Old Testament. Christians cannot approach the Old Testament without some already formed Christian assumptions and beliefs; that is, we read it *as Christians*. It has been a long journey from the beginning of the Old Testament to the advent of Jesus. I do not want to prolong this discussion but, to conclude our study, we need to draw together the threads so that the various parts of this survey can be made into an intelligible unity. After all, the purpose of this book is to help Bible readers to appreciate the structure of God's revelation so that the New Testament's way of linking Jesus to the Old Testament is not a mystery.

> Our faith in Christ means that we will always approach the Old Testament as Christians with certain Christian assumptions.

Christ the fulfiller of all Old Testament scripture

If you now revisit Table 2 in chapter 5 (see p. 52–53), you will be reminded of the proposal there that the three major stages of revelation – Old Testament redemptive history, the recapitulation of these dimensions in the prophets, and the person and work of Jesus – are intimately related. Let me also remind you of our discussion of typology in chapter 4. There is good reason to assert that typology not only exists, but that it is a vital element in the way God reveals his truth in the Bible. The typology lies first of all in the historical revelation; this is then confirmed in the way the prophets recapitulate the terminology of the typology of history; the anti-type is the fulfilment of all these types in Christ. The warning I added to the discussion is that typology, as we express it, must be governed by the theological significance of the type and the anti-type. These must share the same

> Historical and prophetic types often had partial fulfilments but yet pointed forward to the anti-type in Christ.

essential significance in the scheme of God's purposes. The distinction between them lies in the fact that, however 'up front' and final the type may have seemed to its Old Testament contemporaries, it turns out to be only a shadow of the anti-type. But, remember that the shadow was the real means through which the people of that era could grasp the coming reality by faith.

Here are some examples:

- Abraham believed the promises of God and that was accounted to him as righteousness (Genesis 15:6; see also Romans 4:1–25; Galatians 3:1–9).
- The exodus from Egypt was a real saving event for the Israelites who escaped from Egypt, and the second exodus from Babylon was no less a release; but both turn out to be shadows of the true exodus from sin, Satan and death achieved by Christ. Because of the relationship of Jesus Christ to Israel's God, both Paul and Jude can speak of the exodus as involving Jesus (1 Corinthians 10:1–4; Jude 5).
- No suggestion was ever made to Moses that the tabernacle he was told to construct would only be a pale shadow of reality; and Solomon could never have imagined that his magnificent temple would give way to the reality of Christ as the dwelling place of God.
- The covenant promises made to Abraham 'for ever' were seriously received even though they would be given substance by the new covenant in Christ.

The major dimensions of biblical revelation that I have looked at are those set out in Table 2 (p. 52–53). We need to assure ourselves that these are carried through into the idea of Christ the fulfiller. Our study shows that the New Testament teaches clearly that the Old Testament must be interpreted by Christ and not Christ by the Old Testament. While

> Jesus authenticated himself as Messiah by his own authority.

there is an important element of mutual dependence between the two Testaments, the fullness of God's light and truth resides in Christ, the anti-type, and not in the shadowy types in the Old Testament. But, as I have said before, to really understand Christ as the fulfiller we need to understand what he fulfils. Yet, notwithstanding this fact, the ultimate interpreter of truth is Christ.

So, consider this: did the disciples have a checklist of Old Testament characteristics of the predicted Messiah and his kingdom, and then decide that Jesus fitted that pattern? I think not! In fact, the disciples struggled to fit Jesus into their preconceptions of what the Messiah should be like. Of course, it is a complex question, but I suggest that the overwhelming evidence is that Jesus was the Messiah who authenticated himself simply by the authority of who he actually was. His disciples then had to adjust their ideas about the fulfilment of the scriptures to accommodate the real Christ as he revealed himself.

This aspect of the unexpected nature of the Messiah should warn us against preconceived ideas about how the Old Testament promises and predictions would be fulfilled. The answer to the question posed above should be something like this: although there were some prophecies literally fulfilled (virgin birth, place of birth and so on), others came as complete surprises to the disciples (no immediately glorious kingdom in evidence; his suffering and death). The argument I have been making in this study is that the categories or dimensions of God's plan of salvation are transferred to Jesus so that we must look to him and not some supposed events that bypass him for their fulfilment. We must now examine the New Testament evidence for such Christological fulfilment of the Old Testament hope.

Christ and creation

There are two aspects to the relationship of Christ to creation. The first is that the preincarnate Son was the creator. God created by his word; Christ was that Word by whom all things were made; he was the Word who became flesh (John 1:1–3, 14). Paul says it eloquently:

> He [Christ] is the image of the invisible God, the firstborn of all creation. For by him all things were created, in heaven and on earth, visible and invisible, whether thrones or dominions or rulers or authorities – all things were created through him and for him. And he is before all things, and in him all things hold together.
> COLOSSIANS 1:15–17

Nor is Christ the God of the Deists,[12] who believed in a god who simply left his creation to its own devices. Rather, the whole biblical story is of God who is intimately involved in his world even when we are in rebellion. Hebrews speaks of the Son thus:

> But in these last days he has spoken to us by his Son, whom he appointed the heir of all things, through whom also he created the world. He is the radiance of the glory of God and the exact imprint of his nature, and *he upholds the universe* by the word of his power.
> HEBREWS 1:2–3, emphasis mine

The Son not only was intimately involved in creation, but he goes on being the power which holds everything together. Science simply could not happen without Christ as creator and sustainer of the natural universe. The scientists' laws of nature are there because of Christ. Bear in mind this speaks not only of our universe but also of the world of Adam and Eve, of Abraham and of Israel.

The second aspect of Christ's relationship to creation is the fact that he brings the new creation. We have seen how the prophetic idea of renewal extends all the way to the very universe itself: the heavens and the earth (e.g. Isaiah 65:17; 66:22). It may help if we use the words of generation that lie behind the name Genesis. That book refers to the generations, first of the heavens and the

> Science simply could not happen if Christ was not creator and sustainer of the natural universe.

earth, and then of various families. Creation was the generation of the heavens and the earth (Genesis 2:4; see also Genesis 5:1; 6:9; 10:1; 11:10, 27). Genesis 3:14–19 (see also Romans 8:20–23) tells us of the degeneration of all things because of the judgement of God on sin. The whole revelation of God's plan of salvation looks forward to the regeneration of all things, including the heavens and the earth.

The regeneration is proclaimed by Jesus in terms of the fullness of the kingdom. In Matthew 19:28 the Greek word *palingenesis*, which literally translates as 'again-generation' (regeneration) is variously translated as 'the new world' (ESV), 'the regeneration' (KJV) and 'the renewal of all things' (NIV). It refers to the future time of the kingdom and judgement. A verse frequently referred to by those who stress the importance of being born again is 2 Corinthians 5:17, which tells us that 'If anyone is in Christ, he is a new creation'. But this statement is ambiguous since 'he is' is not in the Greek, but is supplied in English translations to construct a complete sentence. Literally the Greek translates as, 'If anyone is in Christ a new creation'. There are grounds from New Testament theology for resolving the ambiguity by recognising that Christ is, in himself, the new creation and we, in union with Christ, also become new creations. Personal regeneration is often regarded as about what happens in believers, but it should be seen as part of the wider regeneration. Both 2 Peter 3:8–13 and Revelation 21:1–5 speak of the new heaven and earth as the consummation of the gospel. It is the making of all things new. This is the ultimate regeneration.

Christ and the covenant

The covenant structures the way a gracious and merciful God articulates his dealings with a rebellious human race. It is about the relationship that God wills to have with his people. The covenant with Noah anticipates the covenant of grace with Abraham. We saw how the covenant dominated the history of the patriarchs and was the basis of the redemptive event of the exodus from Egypt. At the heart of the covenant is everything that goes with God being the God of his people. Such a relationship began in Eden but was lost because of sin. The grace of God is demonstrated in his willingness to bring a people to himself to enjoy fellowship with him.

Because the covenant is a formal way of structuring God's relationship to his people, it actually embraces a number of important aspects of that relationship. Thus, God promised to Abraham a multitude of descendants who would be God's people, live in the promised land and be the means of blessing to the nations of the world. These promises become the basis for the redemptive-saving work of God in the exodus. How the redeemed people should live is conveyed in the Sinai covenant. This was intended to structure Israel's life throughout its history. The Sinai law shows up Israel's rebellion and idolatry so that they are seen to be covenant-breakers.

The one covenant of salvation progresses through a number of expressions until we come to the new covenant in Christ. Thus, Noah's covenant anticipates the covenant of grace made with Abraham. Abraham's covenant necessitates redemption if it is to be in any meaningful way fulfilled, hence the captivity in Egypt and the exodus redemption on the basis of that covenant (Exodus 2:23–25). The Sinai covenant fills out the relationship of God with his people. The constant breaking of the covenant by Israel leads to the removal of all the blessings promised in the covenant and their tangible indicators (land, temple, city, kingship). The prophets promise a new and lasting covenant (e.g. Jeremiah 31:31–34; Ezekiel 16:59–63; 37:24–28).

Behold, the days are coming, declares the Lord, when I will make a new covenant with the house of Israel and the house of Judah, not like the covenant that I made with their fathers on the day when I took them by the hand to bring them out of the land of Egypt, my covenant that they broke, though I was their husband, declares the Lord. But this is the covenant that I will make with the house of Israel after those days, declares the Lord: I will put my law within them, and I will write it on their hearts. And I will be their God, and they shall be my people. And no longer shall each one teach his neighbour and each his brother, saying, 'Know the Lord', for they shall all know me, from the least of them to the greatest, declares the Lord. For I will forgive their iniquity, and I will remember their sin no more.

JEREMIAH 31:31–34

This passage is quoted in Hebrews 8:8–12, and verses 33–34 are quoted in Hebrews 10:15–18. Here the writer is concerned to show that the fulfilment comes as Christ establishes the new covenant. The terminology of Jeremiah must now be understood through the gospel event.

Finally, Jesus himself understood his coming death as the means of sealing the new covenant:

And likewise the cup after they had eaten, saying, 'This cup that is poured out for you is the new covenant in my blood.'
LUKE 22:20

Moses sealed the old Sinai covenant with the blood of the sacrificial oxen by sprinkling blood on the altar and on the people (Exodus 24:3–8). Jesus' sacrificial blood seals and assures the efficacy of the new covenant. This new covenant, then, fulfils all that the old covenant embraced.

Christ and redemption

Two features of redemption dominate the biblical map: the means of redemption and the effects of redemption. The means is constantly portrayed as atoning sacrifice and the effects in terms of rescue from an alien and fatal realm, and restoration into the place of fellowship with God. This redemption I have already identified as an aspect of the covenant. The first hint of this gracious act of God is the promise of redress in Genesis 3:15. Then there is the saving of Noah and his family from the deluge. Once the covenant begins to receive its definitive shape with Abraham, sacrifice emerges as integral to the relationship of God to his people.

The means of redemption continues to be in the shape of the sacrifices, beginning with the Passover lamb, and then with the various kinds of sacrifice stipulated under the Sinai covenant. The instruments and agents of this sacrificial ministry are the altar, the tabernacle and temple, and the priesthood. The 'architecture' (design layout) of both tabernacle and temple graphically and spatially represented the relationship of a reconciled, though sinful, people to a holy God. The sacrifices allowed the priests, as representatives of the people, to come near to God on their behalf. Without priestly mediation, there was no access to God.

The effects of redemption are the initial release from captivity and then entry into the promised land. Then, the atoning sacrifices speak of reconciliation, and enable the representative priest to enter into the presence of God. We saw earlier how the promised land, the temple, the city and the kingship all represent aspects of the restoring of God's people to the blessed state of being with God under his benign rule. Thus, Israel's hope is to be restored to the promised land with a new temple and a new kingship. This terminology is transformed by Jesus in the gospel.

Now Jesus is the mediator of a better covenant than the one that Israel enjoyed (Hebrews 8:1–13). His role as mediator embraces the mediation of God's word, for he is that Word. Along with the prophetic ministry, he enhances the priestly ministry, for he enters into the presence of the Father to make intercession for us; and the kingly ministry as he now rules from heaven. We can now consider the importance of Jesus as God incarnate: God who came among us as a man. He was not a semi-divine man, nor was he a semi-human deity. He was fully God *and* fully man. This is a great mystery, but it is at the heart of the Christian faith. Those who think they have solved, or dissolved, the mystery of the God-Man have actually destroyed the gospel.

Since Jesus is both true God and true man, we can observe the following with regard to his prophetic role. He is the God who speaks. He is the word spoken. But he is also the truly faithful man who hears and obeys that word. And, he is the word that is addressed back to the Father. When it comes to his priestly role, we can see a similarly comprehensive situation. Jesus is God who made us and thus has the right to rule us. He is thus the God against whom all have sinned. Jesus lived as the true and faithful Israelite; as the Son in whom the Father was well pleased. But, he also identified himself with the people of God who have rebelled against God, even though he himself was never a rebel. He suffered as the representative of sinners by being the truly acceptable sacrifice for sin. Thus, he was both priest and sacrifice. He was justified by his resurrection, which demonstrated that he was a righteous human being who could dwell with the Father. These considerations point to the fact that the gospel is the finished and perfect work of Christ. It cannot be repeated. We cannot add to it or take from it. We can only believe it and seek to live consistently with it.

Christ and the dwelling of God

When God gave the Sinai law to Moses it included directions for the tabernacle:

> And let them make me a sanctuary, that I may dwell in their midst. Exactly as I show you concerning the pattern of the tabernacle, and of all its furniture, so you shall make it.
> EXODUS 25:8–9

> I will dwell among the people of Israel and will be their God. And they shall know that I am the Lord their God, who brought them out of the land of Egypt that I might dwell among them. I am the Lord their God.
> EXODUS 29:45–46

When Solomon built the temple in Jerusalem, the Lord spoke to him thus:

> Concerning this house that you are building, if you will walk in my statutes and obey my rules and keep all my commandments and walk in them, then I will establish my word with you, which I spoke to David your father. And I will dwell among the children of Israel and will not forsake my people Israel.
> 1 KINGS 6:12–13

God's constant promise to be with his people, then, is given this added focus that he will dwell among his people. Exiled in Babylon, Ezekiel has a vision of the return of the glory of the Lord to a renewed temple in Jerusalem:

> Son of man, this is the place of my throne and the place of the soles of my feet, where I will dwell in the midst of the people of Israel forever. And the house of Israel shall no more defile my holy name.
> EZEKIEL 43:7

God dwelt with Adam and Eve in Eden. Outside of Eden, it is an act of sheer grace that God chooses a people to be his own, and indicates his dwelling among them. Isaiah's oracle concerning the virgin bearing a son called Immanuel (Isaiah 7:14) probably had its immediate application in Judah close to the time of Isaiah. But Matthew applies it to the coming of Jesus as the true Immanuel. An angelic message comes to Joseph in a dream:

'Joseph, son of David, do not fear to take Mary as your wife, for that which is conceived in her is from the Holy Spirit. She will bear a son, and you shall call his name Jesus, for he will save his people from their sins.' All this took place to fulfil what the Lord had spoken by the prophet: 'Behold, the virgin shall conceive and bear a son, and they shall call his name Immanuel' (which means, God with us).
MATTHEW 1:20–23

John also emphasises the dwelling of God in Jesus:

And the Word became flesh and dwelt among us, and we have seen his glory, glory as of the only Son from the Father, full of grace and truth.
JOHN 1:14

The Greek word that John uses, usually translated as 'dwelt', means literally to dwell in a tent, that is, to 'tabernacle' among us. He is emphasising that the incarnate Son of God fulfils the role of the tent dwelling of God in the wilderness.

The more permanent dwelling of God in Israel was Solomon's beautiful temple. I have stressed the role of the temple as the focal point for God's presence with his people, and as the centre of the priestly ministry of reconciliation through sacrifice. The second temple built in the post-exilic period was renovated and beautified by Herod the Great. All four Gospels record the event when Jesus cleansed the temple and drove out those who used it as a place to make money. This aroused much anger amongst the Jews. Only John records the challenge to Jesus:

> So the Jews said to him, 'What sign do you show us for doing these things?' Jesus answered them, 'Destroy this temple, and in three days I will raise it up.' The Jews then said, 'It has taken forty-six years to build this temple, and will you raise it up in three days?' But he was speaking about the temple of his body. When therefore he was raised from the dead, his disciples remembered that he had said this, and they believed the scripture and the word that Jesus had spoken.
>
> JOHN 2:18–22

Jesus thus diverts attention from the temple made with hands to himself as the fulfiller of the purpose and meaning of the temple: God with us.

The apostles and first Christians soon learned to see in Christ the renewal of the temple so vividly promised by the prophets. The cleansing of the temple by Jesus was an act of judgement showing the awful shortcoming of the earthly temple in fulfilling its purposes. It did not take long for the Jewish Christians to discover that the entire temple theology was fulfilled in Christ. Stephen was stoned to death for pointing this out to unbelieving Jews (Acts 7:44–60). For Paul, the temple takes on a new significance for Jewish and Gentile believers who are united in Christ:

> So then you are no longer strangers and aliens, but you are fellow citizens with the saints and members of the household of God, built on the foundation of the apostles and prophets, Christ Jesus himself being the cornerstone, in whom the whole structure, being joined together, grows into a holy temple in the Lord. In him you also are being built together into a dwelling place for God by the Spirit.
>
> EPHESIANS 2:19–22

So the lines converge. The prophets foretell the day when the Lord God will come to his temple and dwell among his people. Christ, in himself, is God dwelling among us: the perfect union of God and man. By faith, Christians everywhere, and in every age, are united with Christ and so are built into this dwelling place for God. The book of Revelation completes the picture. Although John here reverts to the imagery of Old Testament apocalyptic texts, the message is clear as he describes the heavenly Jerusalem:

> And I saw no temple in the city, for its temple is the Lord God the Almighty and the Lamb.
> REVELATION 21:22

Christ and the day of the Lord

The day of the Lord is a term used by a number of the Old Testament prophets to speak of the future time when God will act both as ultimate saviour and the bringer of final judgement on all the nations, kingdoms and powers that have opposed his kingdom (e.g. Isaiah 2:12; 13:6, 9; Jeremiah 46:10; Ezekiel 13:5; Joel 1:15; 2:1; 3:14; Amos 5:18; Malachi 4:5). Some references are to the day of wrath or judgement (Isaiah 34:8; Zephaniah 1:18; 2:2–3). As I pointed out in chapter 5, the Old Testament does not distinguish between the various comings of the Lord; the day is a time when the promises and threats become reality.

There would be no reason why the Old Testament believers, including the disciples of Jesus, should not think of the day, the coming of the fullness of God's glorious kingdom, as a single event. This would explain some of the bewilderment of the disciples over the way things actually happened in the first coming of Jesus. They struggled with the suffering of the king:

> From that time Jesus began to show his disciples that he must go to Jerusalem and suffer many things from the elders and

chief priests and scribes, and be killed, and on the third day be raised. And Peter took him aside and began to rebuke him, saying, 'Far be it from you, Lord! This shall never happen to you.' But he turned and said to Peter, 'Get behind me, Satan! You are a hindrance to me. For you are not setting your mind on the things of God, but on the things of man.'

MATTHEW 16:21–23. See also MATTHEW 17:12; MARK 8:31–33; 9:12; LUKE 9:22

The death of Jesus was a problem for those who hadn't expected it as part of the day of the Lord. So the two disciples on the road to Emmaus grieved the loss of the one they had hoped 'that he was the one to redeem Israel' (Luke 24:21). The rebuke of the risen Jesus is devastating:

And he said to them, 'O foolish ones, and slow of heart to believe all that the prophets have spoken! Was it not necessary that the Christ should suffer these things and enter into his glory?' And beginning with Moses and all the Prophets, he interpreted to them in all the scriptures the things concerning himself.

LUKE 24:25–27

So the glory would come only after the suffering. They should have known! The books of Moses, the prophets and all the scriptures are, he says, eloquent of this train of events. Jesus, then, has shown that other Old Testament themes cannot be left out of the reckoning of how the day of the Lord comes. The promises of a glorious Son of David ruling cannot be separated from the suffering of the servant of the Lord, especially as seen in Isaiah 42:1–4; 49:1–6; 52:13—53:12.

The death and resurrection of Jesus provides a dynamic to the day of the Lord. First, there is the servant's suffering on behalf of others. The Emmaus road despondency lasted only until they perceived that Christ had risen. The appearance of the risen Christ to the larger group in Jerusalem revived hope that the expected kingdom would now come:

So when they had come together, they asked him, 'Lord, will you at this time restore the kingdom to Israel?' He said to them, 'It is not for you to know times or seasons that the Father has fixed by his own authority. But you will receive power when the Holy Spirit has come upon you, and you will be my witnesses in Jerusalem and in all Judea and Samaria, and to the end of the earth.' And when he had said these things, as they were looking on, he was lifted up, and a cloud took him out of their sight. And while they were gazing into heaven as he went, behold, two men stood by them in white robes, and said, 'Men of Galilee, why do you stand looking into heaven? This Jesus, who was taken up from you into heaven, will come in the same way as you saw him go into heaven.'

ACTS 1:6–11

Here, then, is the sequence: the king suffers and dies; he rises from the dead; he promises the coming of the Spirit to his disciples and declares their ministry to witness; as he ascends to heaven the disciples are reassured of his return in like manner. This is how the Old Testament promises of the day of the Lord are fulfilled: it is at one and the same time a single event and three events. The Lord comes, first, to live among us as a man and to die for us. Second, he sends his Spirit to be present in his church until the final great event. Third, he will come in glory to judge the living and the dead.

When writing to the churches about the final act of the drama of the day of the Lord, Paul can justly speak of the day of Lord or the coming of the Lord. That is, he distinguishes between the three acts: what Christ did for us at his first coming, what his presence by his Spirit now means for our ongoing Christian service, and what will be when he returns in glory (see, for example, Colossians 3:1–4; 1 Thessalonians 4:13—5:11; 2 Thessalonians 2:1–12). Peter also has words about the future day of the Lord (2 Peter 3:1–13). John gives assurance and exhortation in the light of Christ's coming again (1 John 3:1–3; Revelation 1:7).

Jesus Christ, then, brings all the great theological themes of the Old Testament to their fulfilment. All the promises of God find their 'Yes' and 'Amen' in him (2 Corinthians 1:20). The focal point is the resurrection (Acts 13:32–33) according to Paul, because the resurrection is the proof that Jesus has rendered humanity acceptable to God. The resurrection, of course, is part of the ascension of the God-Man to the presence of the Father. All the great themes of the Old Testament are brought to the goal that God has purposed for them. The resurrection-ascension is the Father's 'Amen' to the finished work of Christ on behalf of his people.

Key note
If Jesus is truly the Christ of God, he must be the fulfiller of all God's promises.

Take a moment to reflect…

- Why should the New Testament determine how prophecy and promise are fulfilled?
- If Jesus didn't fulfil all the Old Testament, is he really the Christ?
- Although Jesus is both God and man, consider how his resurrection shows that he was the acceptable Israelite, the true Son of Adam.

Tip: Remember that Jesus was given all authority (Matthew 28:18), and that must include authority to say how the Old Testament is interpreted.

12

D.I.Y.

I will conclude this study by suggesting some practical, do-it-yourself steps in reading the whole Bible as a book about Christ. This summary treatment brings together the practical points made throughout this book in the hope that it will encourage you in several ways. The first point I make in that regard is that the Bible is not totally unmanageable for the non-professional reader. It is not only the academics and theologians who can cope with the task. The second point may seem to be more of a discouragement than the reverse: none of us will ever fully understand the depths of God's revelation this side of glory. That goes for the professional theologians too. But, that should actually be an encouragement because it means that there will always be a freshness and a surprise element in biblical study for those who seek to understand. I can only speak from personal experience. I never cease to be delighted and amazed at new aspects of the truth, new links between texts, new depths to old ideas, even after over 60 years of study of the scriptures.

Before any study of God's word, it makes sense to pray that God will assist your endeavours and, by his Holy Spirit, open up your mind to his word, and make clear his word to your heart and mind.

First step: the big picture

This suggestion will seem like heresy to some who may have been brought up on the idea that Bible reading is a matter of perusing a few verses, and then finding a key pious thought and an identifiable blessing for the day. I have no hesitation in suggesting that, if you have never done it, you should read the Bible from cover to cover like a novel. Even speed read it! Don't stop to question every difficult text or part you can't understand. Press on and get a feeling for the magnificent unity of the Bible. It may take a year or more to complete it, but I dare to suggest to you that, as you pursue this course, you will find that a whole lot of disconnected pieces of biblical information that you have stored over the years of your Bible-reading life begin to make more sense and become more connected.

By way of further encouragement, let me reiterate that you will never get the whole thing so much together that there is nothing more for you to discover. Your sense of the big picture will go on developing and maturing for the rest of your life and, as it does, your sense of wonderment at the magnificence of God's one word will know no bounds.

Second step: close readings

My suggestion above about getting the big picture does not preclude a parallel reading of texts more closely. In fact, you can ensure that it happens by the way you plan your Bible reading. Moreover, you will hear sermons that, hopefully, involve the regular exposition of real texts (not just snippets) of the Bible. In your home group or fellowship the Bible will be studied, so that your diet can consist of both 'big picture' stuff and close reading of texts. So what is involved in close reading?

1 Choose a good 'standard' translation

It really does matter what version you read. There are some versions, usually translations by a single person that can, and sometimes do, distort meaning according to the translator's own convictions. Then there are the 'made simple' versions that often sacrifice accuracy for the sake of simplicity. It is not a good idea to rely on versions that specialise in simplifying everything. These are possibly a good starting point for new Christians, but will not assist good Bible reading for the more mature. The best choice is to get a good modern language translation that is the work of a panel of experts who check on each other's work. I favour the ESV, many prefer the NIV or NRSV.

2 Choose a real unit of text to study

It simply makes sense to take a proper unit for study. Working through a whole book at a time is a good idea. We are, after all, dealing with literature. The individual books have plots or, in the case of Psalms and the wisdom literature, form. They should be dealt with accordingly. Imagine trying to make sense of the last couple of sentences of one of the parables of Jesus. You wouldn't start a mystery novel by turning to the last chapter, so why treat the Bible as some kind of inspirational lucky dip? Sometimes we have to exercise some judgement in the matter, for example, about what constitutes a complete oracle of one of the prophets.

3 Read it for its meaning in context

Even if you are concentrating on only a few verses, these need to be understood in context. If it is part of a statement, who is saying it and why? Does this passage gain meaning from a wider narrative? Beware of hijacking a verse or two to apply in a way that was never intended by the author. Because we are reading the passage in translation, be aware of the fact that different translations can put different slants on meaning. If you have a couple of different translations, it sometimes makes sense to compare their respective renditions of your passage. This is where your sense of the unity of the whole Bible comes in. The context of any passage realistically consists of a series of concentric circles: first, the immediate literary unit; then, the wider context of the chapter or even the whole book; then, ultimately the whole Bible. This may seem to ask a lot, but as you develop your sense of the overall unity of the message of God's kingdom, it becomes easier and easier to propose how the passage you are studying fits into the totality of God's revelation.

4 Probe the passage for its theological meaning

Remember this is God's word about God's deeds in bringing in his kingdom. The Bible is the book dealing with God's acts and we, as humans, must take our rightful place in the pecking order. So, the first question to ask about a unit of text is never, 'What does it say about me?' Rather, we must ask about the way this passage contributes to our understanding of God's great plan of salvation. Since we are primarily concerned in this book with the Old Testament's witness to Christ, this should motivate our questioning of any passage in the Old Testament.

5 Search for the link of any Old Testament passage with Christ

Remember the three stages of revelation in the Bible. These can provide the necessary guide to making the link between the Old Testament and Christ. Don't forget that this needs to be a real theological link, not just an association of ideas. Having recourse to the association of ideas is one of the greatest dangers we face; it is so easy to jump on to some thought about the connection without carefully considering the actual path our thinking has taken. It seems at times that sheer desperation to make the Old Testament text 'Christian' can lead us astray. For example, starting from the account of Nehemiah and the reconstruction of the horse gate in Jerusalem, and moving to Ephesians 6:10–17 (putting on the whole armour of God) on the grounds that soldiers ride horses and wear armour is plainly fanciful.[13] Once we can see how the passage foreshadows Christ, we are in a better position to make some application to those who are in Christ.

6 Ask the question about how we should apply this passage to ourselves

First, I must stress that application to us does not necessarily mean something we must strive to be or do. A passage in the prophets or Psalms may tell us much about the nature of God and about what he has done. Perhaps the bottom line for us is amazement, wonder and praise for who God is. There is no specific practical application; we just gain further insight into what it means for God to be God. Remember, then, that this God has revealed himself most clearly in Jesus, and that it is the God and Father of our Lord Jesus Christ whom we worship.

Then, on the other hand, the Bible is full of practical and personal applications. This does not mean that we can simply bypass Christ by moving from an Old Testament character to us. For example, to take Nehemiah again; it has become popular to expound the book of Nehemiah as principally teaching us about Christian leadership. This may be one useful way to go, but only if this grows out of the actual meaning of the book of Nehemiah. Is the rebuilding of Jerusalem essentially about human leadership, or is there a more important theological point relating to the promises about the city of God and its significance? However faithful a servant Nehemiah was, he only foreshadows the coming of the true builder of Jerusalem and the temple in Jesus. Furthermore, it is the failure of Nehemiah to build the real Jerusalem that drives us forward to find the fulfilment of the prophetic promises of a new Jerusalem in Christ.

7 When you get to the foreshadowed New Testament truths, remember description is not prescription[14]

Remember what we looked at in chapter 5. The New Testament deals with things that are simply facts because they are what has happened in the person and work of Christ when he was here in the flesh. It also deals with the implications of these gospel facts for us in the here and now. Then, finally, it points us to the future when Jesus will return in glory to judge the living and the dead. When the New Testament writers use the indicative verbs,[15] they are simply stating what is. We must distinguish these from the imperatives, the verbs that tell us what should be and how we should act. It is a common error for preachers and teachers of the Bible to take the indicatives and turn them into imperatives.

To give an example: in John 3:1–16 Jesus talks with Nicodemus about being 'born from above' (NRSV). It clearly has Old Testament roots since Jesus suggests that Nicodemus, a Jewish teacher, should understand what he is saying (v. 10). The words of Jesus are indicative; it is easy to mistake verse 7 as imperative because Jesus uses the word 'must'. But he is saying, 'it is necessary to be born again'. He is not commanding Nicodemus to do something, but telling him what must happen if he is to enter the kingdom. Jesus goes on (v. 8) to explain that this new birth is a sovereign work of God's Spirit.

To take another example: sometimes the indicative says something about what is the reality in Christ and then follows this with imperatives telling us how we should respond to this truth. In Colossians 3:3, the indicative is, 'for you have died and your life is hidden with Christ in God'. The imperative that follows in verse 5 is, 'Put to death therefore what is earthly in you.' In Galatians 5:22–24, the indicatives are the fruit of the Spirit; what is a fact for those who walk in the Spirit (v. 16). Paul follows this with the appropriate imperative, 'If we live by the Spirit, let us also walk by the Spirit. Let us not become conceited, provoking one another, envying one another' (vv. 25–26).

* *

I conclude this study with Paul's reminder to the young Timothy that the Old Testament scriptures have been his Bible since his childhood, and have pointed him continually to Christ:

But as for you, continue in what you have learned and have firmly believed, knowing from whom you learned it and how from childhood you have been acquainted with the sacred writings, which are able to make you wise for salvation through faith in Christ Jesus. All scripture is breathed out by God and profitable for teaching, for reproof, for correction, and for training in righteousness, that the man of God may be competent, equipped for every good work.

2 TIMOTHY 3:14–17

Notes

1 Martin Handford's first title is *Where's Wally?* (Walker Books, 1987).
2 Italics in any biblical quotes are mine.
3 You may sometimes hear references to *Tanak*. This is an acronym of the initials of the Hebrew names for the three parts of the Old Testament: Torah, N^evi'im, K^etuvim.
4 The division between the two Testaments is accentuated by the approximately 400 years that elapsed between the end of the Old Testament period and the coming of Jesus. None of the Jewish writings of that in-between period are recognised by the Christian church as inspired scripture and are not included in our Bible. A number of these books are included in the collection known as the Apocrypha. These are useful for gaining insights into the history and culture of the Jews of this period of Hellenistic influence. The Roman Catholic Church accepts the books of the Apocrypha as 'deuterocanonical'. This term originally designated texts received as canonical but not part of the Hebrew Bible.
5 This has evolved into the square Hebrew script that is in use today in inscriptions and printed Hebrew books.
6 Christ (Gk. *Christos*) is the Greek translation of the Hebrew word for Messiah. It means 'the anointed one'.
7 I first used this theme in *Gospel and Kingdom* (Paternoster, 1981), now published as part of *The Goldsworthy Trilogy* (Paternoster, 2000).
8 I have written more extensively about the idea of wisdom in *Gospel and Wisdom* (Paternoster, 1987), now part of *The Goldsworthy Trilogy* (Paternoster, 2000), and in *Proverbs: The tree of life* (Aquila Press, 1993).
9 Parallelism is a frequently used device in Hebrew literature. Essentially, it involves making a statement and then repeating it, maybe with some modifications, but using different words.
10 Two possible exceptions to this rule would be Obadiah and Jonah.
11 This is a frequent rejoinder of those who hold to Dispensational Premillennialism.
12 The Deists were religious rationalists of the 18th century who rejected the idea of revealed truth in favour of a purely reasoned concept of a god who was essentially uninvolved with the world and the affairs of people.

13 I am not making this up! This was the approach of a popular radio
    Bible expositor in the 1960s. In the same sermon he went on to deal
    with the rebuilding of the sheep gate as a passage that took us to
    Jesus the good shepherd.
14 In grammatical terms: an indicative is not an imperative. Because
    something significant is described in a narrative is not necessarily
    the signal for us to try to repeat the event.
15 The 'indicative' is a grammatical term for a verb that states or
    indicates what is.